*Twayne's English Authors Series*

Sylvia E. Bowman, *Editor*

**INDIANA UNIVERSITY**

*P. H. Newby*

*TEAS 176*

# P. H. Newby

# P. H. Newby

### By E. C. BUFKIN

*University of Georgia*

TWAYNE PUBLISHERS

A DIVISION OF G. K. HALL & CO., BOSTON

**Library of Congress Cataloging in Publication Data**

Bufkin, E   C
   P. H. Newby.

   (Twayne's English authors series ; TEAS 176)
   Bibliography:   p. 137-42.
   Includes index.
   1.   Newby, Percy Howard, 1918-   —Criticism and
interpretation.
PR6027.E855Z6   823'.9'14   74-22324
ISBN   0-8057-1414-6

PR
6027
. E855
Z6

MANUFACTURED IN THE UNITED STATES OF AMERICA

66932

M.E.M.
J.L.S.
F.F.S.

*London*
*1968*

# Contents

# About the Author

E. C. Bufkin is a member of the Department of English at the University of Georgia, Athens, where he teaches courses in modern literature. A native of Mississippi, he was educated at the universities of Tulane, Harvard, and Vanderbilt (from which he holds a Ph.D.). In addition to articles and reviews in various journals, his publications include *The Twentieth-Century Novel in English: A Checklist*.

# Preface

The reputation of P. H. Newby has ranked high among present-day English novelists since the appearance of his first novel, *A Journey to the Interior*, in 1945. Only scant serious, extensive critical attention, however, has been devoted to him in either England or the United States. In view of both the quantity of his body of work and its consistently fine quality, a comprehensive examination of it is surely overdue. To make such an examination is the purpose of this first book about him.

Such a study is meant to assist readers in reaching a clearer understanding of Newby's novels, which, as has often been pointed out, are sometimes baffling or obscure. Moreover, the study will introduce to American readers those novels by Newby that have not been published in this country and are, consequently, difficult to come by. One of those, *A Step to Silence*, is particularly important for understanding and more fully appreciating its sequel, *The Retreat*, the only one of the two which has been published in the United States.

The method of this book is descriptive and analytic. The first chapter deals briefly with the author's background and presents an overview of his leading themes and characteristic techniques. The following chapters analyze individually each of his novels in order of publication. In each instance in the text where page numbers are cited, the reference is to the American editions of Newby's novels, with the exception of *Mariner Dances*, *The Snow Pasture*, *A Step to Silence*, and *The Loot Runners*, which were published only in London.

I should like to record here my appreciation to several people. To James Korges, editor in chief of *Critique: Studies in Modern Fiction*, I am grateful for permission to make use of an article of mine which first appeared in that journal. To Gerald Chambers, for his generous help in a straitened time, I owe a special word of thanks.

P. H. NEWBY

For her frequent and unfailingly resourceful assistance, I cordially thank Mrs. Christine Burroughs of the University of Georgia Libraries. And for criticisms and suggestions about this little book while it was slowly taking shape I am most particularly indebted to C. A. Beaumont, *magister rhetoricae*.

E. C. BUFKIN

*University of Georgia*
*Athens, Georgia*

# Acknowledgments

For permission to quote, acknowledgment is made to the following:

P. H. Newby and Jonathan Cape for *Agents and Witnesses, A Journey to the Interior, Mariner Dances, The Snow Pasture, A Step to Silence*.

From *The Young May Moon* by P. H. Newby. Copyright 1950 by P. H. Newby. Reprinted by permission of Alfred A. Knopf, Inc.

From *A Season in England* by P. H. Newby. Copyright 1951 by P. H. Newby. Reprinted by permission of Alfred A. Knopf, Inc.

From *The Retreat* by P. H. Newby. Copyright 1953 by P. H. Newby. Reprinted by permission of Alfred A. Knopf, Inc.

From *The Picnic at Sakkara* by P. H. Newby. Copyright, ©, 1955 by P. H. Newby. Reprinted by permission of Alfred A. Knopf, Inc.

From *A Guest and His Going* by P. H. Newby. Copyright, © 1959 by P. H. Newby. Reprinted by permission of Alfred A. Knopf, Inc.

From *Revolution and Roses* by P. H. Newby. Reprinted by permission of Harold Ober Associates Incorporated. Copyright, ©, 1957 by P. H. Newby.

From the book *The Barbary Light* by P. H. Newby. Copyright, ©, 1962 by P. H. Newby. Reprinted by permission of J. B. Lippincott Company.

From the book *One of the Founders* by P. H. Newby. Copyright, ©, 1965 by P. H. Newby. Reprinted by permission of J. B. Lippincott Company.

From the book *Something to Answer For* by P. H. Newby. Copyright, ©, 1968 by P. H. Newby. Reprinted by permission of J. B. Lippincott Company.

# Chronology

1918    Percy Howard Newby born June 25 in Crowborough, Sussex.

1936-   At St. Paul's College, Cheltenham.
1938

1939    Enlisted in Royal Army Medical Corps.

1939-   In France with British Expeditionary Force.
1940

1941-   In Egypt with Middle East Force.
1942

1942-   Lecturer in English Literature at Fouad I University, Cairo.
1946

1945    Married Joan Thompson; *A Journey to the Interior.*

1946    Received Atlantic Award in Literature for *A Journey to the Interior;* settled in Buckinghamshire.

1947    *Agents and Witnesses; The Spirit of Jem.*

1948    *Mariner Dances;* received Somerset Maugham Award for *A Journey to the Interior.*

1949    *The Snow Pasture; The Loot Runners.*

1949-   Member of the British Broadcasting Corporation Talks
1958    Department.

1950    *The Young May Moon; Maria Edgeworth.*

1951    *A Season in England; The Novel 1945-1950.*

1952    *A Step to Silence;* visited the United States.

1953    *The Retreat.*

1955    *The Picnic at Sakkara.*

1957    *Revolution and Roses.*

1958    *Ten Miles from Anywhere and Other Stories;* controller, British Broadcasting Corporation Third Programme.

1959    *A Guest and His Going.*

1962    *The Barbary Light.*

1965    *One of the Founders.*

1968    *Something to Answer For.*

1969    Received *Yorkshire Post* Fiction Award and Booker Fiction Prize for *Something to Answer For.*

1970    Controller, British Broadcasting Corporation Radio Three.

1971    Director of Programmes, British Broadcasting Corporation Radio.

CHAPTER 1

# Prelude

Seeke wee then our selves in our selves; for as
Men force the Sunne with much more force to passe,
By gathering his beames with a christall glasse;

So wee, If wee into our selves will turne,
Blowing our sparkes of vertue, may outburne
The straw, which doth about our hearts sojourne.
                                                                        —John Donne

## I  The World of the Artist

P. H. NEWBY has stated that since an early age he has had
no other serious ambition than to be a writer.[1] The
publication of A Journey to the Interior in December, 1945, marked
the realization of that ambition and the beginning of a successful
career.[2] Now, nearly thirty years later, he is still writing and has
produced a considerable body of work: novels, novels for juveniles,
short stories, and works of criticism. Among other notable English
novelists whose careers began, like Newby's, after World War II —
Angus Wilson, William Golding, Iris Murdoch, Muriel Spark — he
has few superiors even though his books may not be so well or so
widely known as some of theirs.

His life, insofar as it is directly relevant to his career as a novelist,
may be viewed as falling into three periods. The first of these ex-
tends from his birth in 1918 to his entering the army in 1939.
Because his father had "an itch to keep moving," the family lived in
various parts of England and South Wales; and Newby's earliest
memories are of the "contrast between green fields and the in-
dustrial darkness of the mining valleys."[3] The place to which he
says he owes allegiance is Worcestershire, where one of his grand-
fathers had a market garden and did chimney sweeping and where
Newby received his early education. The second period is that of

World War II, most of which he spent in Egypt. Living there, he has commented, "outside Europe and the Christian tradition was probably the best thing that could have happened to me as a writer."[4] The third period began with the publication of *A Journey to the Interior* and his return to England in 1946. Since 1949 he has been prominently associated with the British Broadcasting Corporation, continuing to write and publish all the while.

Each of Newby's novels is short, stringent, highly organized, and heavily patterned; he neither writes nor admires the expansive type of novel that Henry James termed "fluid puddings." Newby has described modern novelists as being of two kinds, the historian (such as C. P. Snow) and the poet (Iris Murdoch).[5] The historian is concerned with "merely ordering and transcribing experience in narrative prose," but the poet transcends the level of "merely representing the real world." The poetry of a book is its comedy and tragedy, but the satiric and the visionary are also poetry.[6] Newby himself is, according to his own classifications, a poet; and Richard Church's remark that "not since the death of Virginia Woolf has the art of the novel been practised by so deliberate an artist"[7] quite aptly summarizes Newby's position among his contemporaries.

Despite the unique individuality of his writing, Newby's lineage from the great tradition of the English novel is easy to trace. To Dickens, "a very conscious literary artist," he admits a large debt,[8] which is most obvious, perhaps, in his creation of humorous, eccentric, and grotesque characters. A constant concern with moral behavior links Newby with George Eliot as well as with Henry James. From James also, of course, stem Newby's artistic conscience and his preoccupation with technique and form.

Newby has commented that he does not read D. H. Lawrence or James Joyce because their powerful influence might lead to emulation.[9] Nonetheless, the influence of Lawrence in particular is noticeable in Newby's novels, especially the earlier ones; and it appears in the descriptions of place and of nature which often, as in Lawrence, function as structural and thematic symbols. Lawrence's influence is also to be seen in many of Newby's principal characters and in his attitude toward them, which, although not voiced outright, is nevertheless clearly perceivable. Like Lawrence, Newby portrays his characters both physically and psychologically—they are always remarkably *there*, visually and emotionally; and one can say that Newby, like Lawrence, rejects the "old stable ego" of character for the individual passing through "allotropic states." Walter Allen, who has called attention to these Lawrentian practices and effects in Newby, has observed that he too "catches his characters at the very moment of living, before the intellect has had time to intervene and generalize the moment experienced."[10] Newby has also expressed affinities with E. M. Forster, with whom the younger man was too long compared as an inferior imitator. Newby has termed himself a "liberal in my thinking, in the sense that E. M. Forster is"; and he dislikes "absolute beliefs, dogma."[11] But this influence, even that of *A Passage to India* on *The Picnic at Sakkara* which Newby has acknowledged, can be overemphasized.[12] Indeed, the predecessor with whom Newby can most illuminatingly be compared is Joseph Conrad, and the centers of Newby's novels may even at times contain a vapor rather than a jewel, as Forster once said of Conrad. The influence of Conrad is unmistakable from the outset in *A Journey to the Interior*, with its mythic quest for self-knowledge so strongly reminiscent in many ways of "Heart of Darkness," but the principal manifestation of Conrad's influence is not technical. Newby hardly ever, for instance, uses a first-person narrator or multiple narrators; and his arrangement of chronology is almost always without exception straightforward.

Yet Newby's novels may appear on the surface to be more traditional, less experimental, than they really are. The point should be emphasized, as one critic has done, that Newby is, importantly, a serious technical innovator.[13] Because of the nature of his material, he often works his novels out on a level of abstraction that could not well be represented in realistic terms. His plots transcend the realistic, and the reader has to accept their action for its significance, not for its verisimilitude, in much the way he accepts, for example, the literal action of the last plays of Shakespeare. A passage in *A Journey to the Interior* may be used to describe this method of presentation: "The words that were uttered were like beads that a woman will finger as she talks — the real conversation was carried on at a higher level, without words" (184–185).

External action, then, is metaphorical as well as literal, and it dramatizes the inner states of the characters. Prose functions as poetry, providing symbolic implications and suggestions that expose

meaning on more than one level; and for the structuring of such
narrative Newby employs an innovative approach. In the first chapter of *The Barbary Light,* which affords an excellent illustration of
Newby's narrative methods, the protagonist Owen is in bed with his
mistress, Alex, who is exploring his body with her hands and his past
life with questions. This action serves to foreshadow, at the same
time that it initiates, the thematic exploration of Owen that is made
throughout the novel—not only by the characters themselves but by
the reader as well. In this chapter, Alex moves back and forth from
the waking to the sleeping state; and, in doing so, she intermingles
the real and the illusory, appearance and reality, which are the
thematic subject-matter of the whole novel. But Alex also intermingles her own memories with Owen's reported memories of his
boyhood; and, with this technical conjoining, Newby stresses by
ironic contrast the elements of isolation and solitude that constitute
the major aspect of Owen's predicament. Here, as Owen says, only
memory is identity. That the reader will be, in this opening chapter,
slightly confused on a first reading is the precise intent; for the rest
of the novel will, like the Barbary light in Africa to which both hero
and reader progress, clarify this particular situation and define the
relationship of Owen with the other characters (and himself). Thus
technique, looking forward while gazing backward, formulates the
hero's problem; structures the complex design of narrative; and in-
volves the reader himself directly in an amazingly original manner.
Form and manner seldom blend more effectively into a unified
whole.

## II  *Questers*

All of Newby's novels are concerned with an isolated, bewildered
hero who is more often than not a wanderer. Very few of his characters are attached professionally, emotionally, or domestically to a
given place. Even if some are so attached, all of them move about
physically just as they move about psychologically; the impression is
that of a world of restlessness and impermanence. The most constant element in Newby's novels is the journey—literal,
metaphysical, and mythic; and all of his protagonists are traveling
questers. These isolated, bewildered characters find themselves in
extreme situations; as one critic has pointed out, the novels,
"though suppressed into a show of calm," are all "sensational":

they are about "the clash of loyalties, the explosive pressures of society, the consuming urge . . . for a man to identify himself to himself."[14] The involved questers' search is a spiritual adventure; they seek not for tangibles but for intangibles—religious, moral, psychological; and their dilemmas and problems are fundamentally personal, not public. As they seek, the questers move away from the disorder of innocence, misunderstanding, or alienation to the order of experience, knowledge (of self and others), or reconciliation. The significance of this progression resides in the moral positives that it dramatizes, endorses, and celebrates.

Not one of Newby's novels is without this movement, which is the tripartite pattern of archetypal myth. Each protagonist undergoes a separation, a climactic experience leading to a spiritual renewal and integration, and a return.[15] Most often this quest-journey into self—into the interior—is actual as well as psychological, just as it is in the first novel. The mythic experience thus becomes a redemptive experience, and it provides the moral norm by which the protagonist, in meeting the tests of that experience, is judged. It is significant that, unlike those of many of his contemporaries, Newby's characters are redeemed; they save themselves from isolation, despair, and spiritual death instead of driving toward the catastrophe of alienation. Only twice, in *Agents and Witnesses* and in *A Season in England,* does the Newby protagonist fail.

### III   *The World of Imagination*

Newby's view of life is not without Conradian tints; for, as he sees the human situation, it is "desperate": "We're terribly vulnerable, weak animals in a cold and hostile universe. . . . Life is precarious. Life is hell and this is much more fundamental about a man than any thought about the particular social status he might happen to occupy."[16] In this situation the one annealing power, and a concept central to all of Newby's fiction, is the imagination. It serves for him, in his view of experience, both a literary and an extraliterary function; and the "deliberate act of the imagination" (a phrase he uses in *A Step to Silence*) is the means toward effective action in the real world as well as in the world of art. The end toward which such an act of the imagination can lead is the cessation of isolation, of loneliness, and of the sense of alienation—a Conradian solidarity of mankind.

This concept of the imagination derives from Percy Bysshe Shelley, as Newby has explained in "The World of Imagination," an essay essential to the understanding of his work.[17] Man sees more, Newby writes, by the light of the imagination than any other human faculty, even reason. " 'A man to be greatly good,' said Shelley, 'must imagine intensively and comprehensively; he must put himself in the place of another and of many others; the pains and pleasures of his species must become his own.' " This quotation, says Newby, defines the goal to which the novelist must commit himself; he thereby defines the moral nature of the art of the novel. "The great instrument of moral good," asserted Shelley, "is the imagination."

The characters of fiction, Newby continues in this same essay, can enlighten the sensitive reader. They demonstrate to him the "diversity of humanity" and confirm that men "are not alone but one of many millions"; they indicate that they "are not unique, or peculiar, or strange, because everyone is unique and everyone is peculiar and everyone is strange." The imagination has produced this sense of identity with others, and another name for the imagination is love, Newby's abiding theme.

The effects of imagination which literature creates upon and in a reader can and should therefore be sought, by implication, in the real world, where so many are, or feel, alone. The novelist, drawing upon the real world for his material, includes in his fictional world, for moral edification and for enlightenment, the powers, the workings, and the effects of deliberate actions of the imagination. Literature, in establishing through imagination this sense of the identity of all men, the best as well as the worst, will in the end have a most benevolent result: "it lifts us up to a point of splendour where there is no such thing as an individual sorrow or even an individual guilt, but only a holy sense of the thread of common humanity which runs through each and every one of us."

## CHAPTER 2

# *Desert and Island*

NEWBY has commented, with considerable earnestness and conviction, on the moral situation of the years immediately following World War II and its effect on fiction. The "quality of a work of fiction," he says, "depends on the quality of thought of the times in which it is written. The great novelists of the past wrote well because they thought well: anyone writing fiction to-day who wishes to do so with effect must first make up his mind just where he stands, as a human being, at this moment of history. It is no longer possible," he continues, to write "novels of the first importance" which ignore wars and revolutions or "the deeper issues, the bewilderment, the confusion of loyalties, the search for belief and faith." And he states that "destruction, civilisation in ruins, man's moral degradation and spiritual poverty" are the "theme which forces itself on to the novelist's attention these days."[1] In his first two novels, *A Journey to the Interior* (1945) and *Agents and Witnesses* (1947), Newby turned directly to these "deeper issues" and to the themes of man's moral degradation, spiritual poverty, and quest for belief.

## I  A Journey to the Interior

As the symbolism and the imagery reveal, *A Journey to the Interior* concerns a quest for self-knowledge and, especially, for resurrection—the triumph of life over death. The hero, Winter, is sent by the oil company which employs him to its outpost in the desert sultanate of Rasuka. He has actually been sent there to recuperate from an attack of typhoid; but, as the result of the recent death of his wife Joyce in childbirth, he is as weak emotionally as he is weak physically: he is "a tangle of unresolved emotions" (56). He meets among the colonials in Rasuka a young woman, Nellie, who resembles Joyce, and eventually he begins an affair with her. He also becomes fascinated—haunted—by repeated talk about an ec-

21

centric man named Rider who has recently disappeared into the interior. And he becomes unwittingly involved with Hebechi, a native
who, after an attempt at murder, also flees to the interior. Ostens-
ibly to go after Hebechi and to look for Rider, Winter makes a
journey himself to the interior; but he finds neither of the men. He
and his party, among whom is the young native boy Osman, are attacked; and Osman is killed. Profoundly affected by the boy's
death, Winter returns to Rasuka; finds that he is fully recovered,
physically and emotionally; and rejoins Nellie, whom he is apparently going to marry.

Winter's physical condition is but an outward manifestation or
symbol of his emotional or inner condition. With a technique that
appears to be simple but is in reality extremely complex, Newby
works out his hero's quest on several corresponding levels simultaneously. Winter's name, obviously symbolical, initiates a system
of season imagery that runs through the novel and connotes at once
the dead, unproductive season and the spiritual poverty of Winter's
soul. This condition has been caused in great part by the death of
Joyce, who, by means of a photograph, is associated with spring: "It
was a photograph of spring-like happiness. It was Winter's dead
wife" (71). Thus Joyce represents spring or summer and life
(paradoxically, since she is dead); Winter represents winter and
death (paradoxically too, since he is alive).

Nellie looks like Joyce, so much so that Winter, at their second
meeting, is almost deceived into believing that the living woman is
his wife: " 'Then you are not dead,' he was shouting silently, 'not
dead and I knew it all the time. There is no death' " (80). Significantly, because of the connection of light with spring, Nellie is
seen sitting in a column of light that is coming into the room
through a skylight; and she reminds Winter of the photograph of
Joyce: "But the photograph had not the reality of the unseen image
in his heart which was his wife's face graced by his own love, nor
the startling objectivity of this pale woman sitting at the foot of her
column of crystal. For both faces were the same, the image in his
heart and this. The photograph could say nothing half as effective"
(80).

Not only do the two women look alike, but also they use the same
perfume—the perfume, like the light, is easily associated with
summer, as the omniscient narrator points out: "The unbelievable

fact was that she was wearing the same perfume that his wife used to wear—a perfume . . . redolent of summer ripeness and warm, moth-like evenings" (133). Association thus blends the two women, the living and the dead, into one. Winter's reunion with Nellie after his journey to the interior symbolizes his recovery—the recovery of his dead wife vicariously through the living woman and the recovery, or restoration, of his own life through the feminine-spring (or feminine-summer) principle of birth and growth.

The season imagery dovetails with, and is supported by, another system of imagery, that of sleep, which implies the appearance-reality motif. At the outset, Newby indicates that Winter is symbolically dead by equating his condition with sleep. Winter reflects that "one day he would awake, he knew" (19). Winter is, of course, the dormant season: what is seemingly dead is only sleeping; and death, in Christian phraseology, is but a sleep. The experience which Winter undergoes functions to awaken him, to bring him back to life, to resurrect him; and, after his journey, the sleep imagery is used to reveal this fact: "Winter had awakened" (154).

Until awakened, Winter has lived symbolically, therefore, not in the world of reality but in the sleeping, dreaming world of appearance. His confusion of the two worlds is due to both his physical illness, typhoid fever, and his emotional-spiritual illness. By the time he arrives in Rasuka, he has already become confused; for by then his custom was to regard his dead wife "as the reality and himself as the illusion. . . . Intangible, unsolid, he thought. It is the dream curtain behind which I shall suddenly come upon her in a burst of sunshine. All was a dream and the ordinary chances of life had no impact" (19). Shortly afterward, Winter has a real dream, a subconscious projection, on the literal narrative level, of the turmoil within him; and the effect of the dream causes him to think of reality in terms of a bad dream: "Immediately he went into an oppressed dream in which he was chained and could not move, was about to be struck and could not avoid the blow, was in great danger and yet paralyzed. He awoke suddenly. . . . The moon had gone, but between him and the stars he was aware of the black shape of a human head. Coming out of his sleep, his spirit naked against this unknown quality, Winter was terrified. It was the cold, unreasoning fear of a nightmare" (69).

Ultimately, the season and the sleep imagery coalesce with

another, the major, system of imagery in the novel: that of religion, especially the resurrection. This coalescence is effected through the fast of Ramadan, which occurs in the novel just prior to Winter's journey to the interior and which is greatly responsible for the effect it has in motivating that journey. The word *Ramadan*, which literally means "the hot month," indicates the coming of the warmth of summer; thus it foreshadows the change of Winter, as man and as symbolical season, which takes place during the journey. Furthermore, the fast of Ramadan, which seems to have been influenced by Jewish traditions, functions in this novel as a counterpart to the Day of Atonement. For the fast both inspires Winter's journey and foreshadows his spiritual reconciliation, an atonement that results in his rebirth and new life—spring and summer. Like both pagan gods and Christ, then, Winter is resurrected in the spring, which is both occasion and symbol of regeneration.

The resurrection imagery begins in the very first sentence of *A Journey to the Interior:* "On the third day the land rose out of the sea." "Third day" and "rose" suggest the resurrection of Christ and announce, indirectly, the theme of the novel. Land and sea function as traditional symbols of safety and danger or, more explicitly, life and death, respectively. Winter's main journey, that to the interior, is prefaced by a voyage (or sea journey) which brings him to the location where that larger journey will ultimately occur and will prepare him, in turn, for "that other journey . . . into the future" (276) which he is to undertake at the end of the novel.

Winter's emotional—and spiritual—illness is what he has come to the desert seeking a cure for: " 'I've got romantic ideas about Rasuka,' said Winter. 'That was why I came. Not so much because of health. . . . But I thought that in bareness and nakedness there would be some sense of . . . primitive origins. I thought that I could get hold of something simple and essential in myself' " (30-31). The cause of his nonphysical illness is his inability to face death; he even "feared any talk of death" (160). On the ship that brings him to Rasuka are a woman and her husband; when the husband suddenly and unexpectedly dies, the wife's violent reaction and her overwrought recognition of death contrast with Winter's inability to react to his wife's death. Benumbed, he has felt no grief—"since her sudden death there had been time for grief but no grief had come"—and he has not, like the sobbing woman, wept:

"How was it that he had not wept . . . ?" Winter "could envy the woman the spontaneity of her grief. She, at least, had recognized the enemy [death] immediately and had known no confusion. Her tears were washing away that which still remained in Winter's breast as an obstruction" (19).

He accepts only the appearance, not the reality, of his wife's death, as he himself admits: "It has never become real for me, her death" (179). The strands of imagery here become, like Winter's emotions, entangled. In the interior he at last acknowledges the reality of death; then "he had awakened. . . . He had discovered death" (254). Upon the murder of his guide, the boy Osman, Winter at last feels grief for the first time; as one of the members of his party says, "It is not fear that man [Winter] is feeling. . . . It is grief" (248). Winter recognizes that "the dead had their own providence," and he mourns for all deaths—his wife's, Osman's, Rider's, even his own. The tears—rejuvenating therapeutic water, working as part of the spring imagery—finally come; and, at the end, Winter "had mourned and the impediment had been dissolved out by his tears. At last they had come" (276). And so they have contributed to the spring that is Winter's resurrection.

The religious imagery surrounds, like hoops, the journey to the interior which Winter makes to find Rider, a singular man who is a god and a Christ-figure. The native Hebechi says that Rider "was a god" (160), and one of the colonials at Rasuka says of Rider: "He was a revolutionary. He didn't care for us and what was right or wrong. He had his own ways of measuring right and wrong. They were not our ways. He stood away from us. You just had to admire him. He was like Christ" (197).

Newby compares Winter with Rider and so, just as Joyce and Nellie are symbolically one woman, the two men, Rider and Winter, become symbolically one man. One of the Englishmen living in Rasuka points out the connection to Winter: "Don't you see how people identified you with Rider? . . . There was the gift of food—bread left on your doorstep. Didn't you guess? Hebechi came to you when he wanted advice. He did not think of going to anyone else" (200). Consequently, in seeking Rider, Winter is actually seeking both himself—his *real* self—and Christ. Although he does not find Rider, he comes to the firm conclusion that Rider is dead (as he himself has in effect been until this journey to the interior):

"'No, he is dead,' said Winter positively. 'Rider is dead. Of that there is not the slightest doubt'" (255).

Winter, whose condition is comparable to the infertile desert land, has found in the interior—by extension, his own inner self—the reality of death. And so, though he does not find the godlike, Christlike Rider, he symbolically finds Christ in the recognition of death. For complete belief in Christ as God requires belief in His actual physical death as man. To accept the concept of death is to accept, at the same time, the concept of life; and Winter, now momentarily a Christ-figure himself, accepts death and, paradoxically, attains life. In this manner, he transcends his emotional and spiritual frustrations; he finds atonement, resurrection, and life in the interior; and he returns to Rasuka a different, because changed, man—a fact symbolized physically by the beard he had grown (representative of both physical and spiritual energy and fertility) and spiritually by "the distraught kind of happiness that was radiating from his face" (275). The point is explicitly made with a Pauline allusion[2] that clinches the salvific imagery: "The last signs of his illness had gone away. . . . He felt like a new man. He had been re-born" (274).

## II   Agents and Witnesses

*Agents and Witnesses,* set like *A Journey to the Interior* in a fictional region in the Near East, is in most other respects a contrast to the first novel. Both technically and thematically, the second novel is more complex and more sophisticated than its predecessor. Although it contains elements of farce and several humorous episodes, *Agents and Witnesses* is a work of profound seriousness. The foundation on which it is built is the Christian ethic of goodwill and selfless service to one's fellowman, and its very title is redolent of Christian action and testimony.

The innovation of the novel is Newby's oblique method, through the use of irony, of making a positive statement through negative example. In contrast with *A Journey to the Interior,* which makes a positive statement through affirmative example, alienation replaces reconciliation, death replaces life, in *Agents and Witnesses.* The world and the characters of this second novel lack a viable system of spiritual belief, and the author shows what happens to people who not only inhabit such a world but make it what it is through action and inaction alike. The Mediterranean island Sankilos, where all of the action occurs, functions with its international population as a microcosm of the modern world. The protagonist, Pierre Bartas, is not only its Everyman figure in search of belief, meaning, and purpose; he is also its scapegoat.

Pierre is a young French architect living in Sankilos. The turning point in his life, brought about by a fortuitous and ambiguous event, occurs when he is returning from a visit to the malaria-infested mountain province of Kole. Pegia, a doctor who has been in Kole working to control the disease, leaves with Pierre in his car, which goes out of control and heads over a cliff. Pierre jumps out and shouts for the doctor to jump too; but Pegia, though he has time to do so, does not leave the car and falls to his death in it.

One of Pierre's clients is the Turk Soureili, who decides to run for President of Sankilos. His son Nabil determines, in order to achieve his own ambitions, to obtain the presidency for his father by various revolutionary means and then take control himself. Nabil's activities form a second plot in the novel, and the two plots are connected by the two Keats sisters: Marthe, who becomes an admiring follower of Nabil; and Anna, who falls in love with Pierre. Both plots are resolved when Nabil's forces storm the city to take over the government. Pierre decides to join the insurgents and goes in search of Nabil. From the building in which they have taken cover, Nabil and Marthe see him approaching. Because Nabil thinks Pierre to be the government agent who killed Pegia and mistrusts him and because Marthe despises Pierre for his mistreatment of her sister, Nabil shoots and kills him.

Sankilos is a place where "the morality is upside down" (115). Conditions on the island reflect man's degradation and spiritual poverty, and they are worsened by both man and nature. The mountainous provinces are plagued by deadly mosquitoes; the city, by rats. Conflict and ignorance exist on all levels of society, and "all social problems become political issues, questions of personal enmity and prestige" (32). Moreover, "religion as such had ceased to be a moral driving force"; consequently, "the only service in which self-denial was not reprehensible" was "the acquisition of money"—of which creed Soureili, the wealthiest man on the island, is the "high priest" (108). Wealth has created its own standards of morality—"Nabil was . . . so immensely wealthy that he could do

no wrong" (185). Good intentions, good works, self-sacrifice are
significant only if they yield a desired profit or reward. The material
object is of value only for itself or for power, not for its spiritual or
esthetic manifestations. Pegia, who speaks out against "the rotten
conditions in the country, the indifference, the corruption, the
mercenariness," longs for a "moral renaissance." "How," he asks,
"can men fail to be good when there are such opportunities for
goodness?" (114–115). Yet the characters who people this world
"fail to be good" because they are almost without exception morally
weak. Most of them are repulsively fat, and this unattractive
physical trait, paralleling their cupidity and selfishness, reflects the
moral turpitude and debasement that they perpetuate as agents or
tolerate as witnesses.

The reader's moral censure and disapprobation of the characters
are gained and enforced through an indirect method. Certain of
them are associated by name and by action with archetypal biblical
personages, and this ironic device of juxtaposed contrast discloses
and defines the characters' spiritual failure. This parodic technique
thus serves as moral criticism since the discrepancy not only displays
the reality but simultaneously measures its distance from the ideal.
For example, Marthe recalls Martha, who is noted for her hospitable attention to Christ and her service to the needy. Marthe in
her connection with Nabil becomes an ironic inversion of her
biblical counterpart; and, by extension, Nabil becomes, through his
relationship with Marthe, an anti-Christ figure. Marthe sees in
Nabil a great and powerful leader whose revolutionary campaign to
gain control of Sankilos will result in material wealth which she can
abundantly share. She acts as hostess for him when he entertains
military officers, and she subscribes to his creed of personal and
political duplicity: "Everybody our enemies, yet we the friends of
all" (187). To Martha, Christ said, "I am the resurrection and the
life"; instead of being such, on the human level, to Marthe and the
people of Sankilos, Nabil is a betrayer, a tyrant, a destroyer of men,
and a murderer.

Pegia is a contrasting parallel to Nabil. Likened to a saint, the
bearded doctor—than whom "a less selfish and kinder man never
lived" (130)—enacts (up to a point) the example of the true Christ
against a "tired, faded, allegorical landscape" (111). He travels
about the provinces working among the poor, stricken peasantry

("They're just sheep" [63]) and distributing loaves to them because "I thought I might save you" (124). In one scene, he addresses the peasants while standing on a "flat-topped stone" and promises them, "I shall come back in three days" (125). (In the farcical and satirical episode of Pegia's funeral, Soureili's materialistic cynicism turns the burial into a parody of Christ's resurrection: "Soureili could not look at the coffin without trying to imagine what was inside it. Perhaps there was nothing at all! Oh yes, he knew that happened sometimes" [148].)

The physician Pegia has become discouraged, however, in his work and has succumbed to a "terrible apathy" and a "sense of futility" (117, 122). "There could not be any *rightness* where there was no success!" he thinks (135). Even he the physician, then, is infected with the spiritual disease of Sankilos and cannot heal himself. Weak in faith and perseverance, he abandons his work and opts for a passive death which, though apparently suicide, is technically not self-destruction. At this point, the Pegia-Christ parallel breaks off, leaving the doctor in an unfavorable light. His role in the experience of Pierre becomes ultimately ironic since, speaking of noble and high actions, he cannot finally adhere to the code of Christian endeavor which he has embraced and so, unwittingly, he leads Pierre on toward his own death. Pegia becomes, thematically, a failed Christ.

The other character subjected to this kind of ironic treatment is Pierre, the principal character. His story, which provides an encircling frame for the novel, moves from chaos through confusion back to chaos; the structure is so handled that it is finally unified through the logical, but ironic, culmination of the episodes of Pierre's life. Although he comes to Sankilos on a materialistic quest for money, his experience turns, almost in spite of himself, into a spiritual quest. As an artist, he is at first in search of meaning in life; gradually, he gropes amid moral muddlement for the meaning *of* life. In the world of Sankilos, where no "moral driving force" is available to impel him, Pierre can conceive of the goal of his quest for spiritual meaning in only the vaguest terms. The reader, who sees him as a wanderer in a confused world, appreciates his aspirations and efforts to come to some kind of terms with ultimate significances: "One *had* to believe that there was a significance somewhere," he says (137).

The beauty of the novel is due in large measure to Newby's show-
ing how, in Pierre's case, character is fate. The reason for the failure
of his zigzagging journey toward meaning lies within Pierre
himself: he is the self-centered man who would gain the whole
world but loses his soul. As his name ("Peter") hints, he functions as
a disciple, but he is a disciple looking for a master.[3] The points of
similarity between Pierre and St. Peter are noteworthy. In the scene
in which we first see him, Pierre is looking for his key. He is closely
associated with churches; of one that he is restoring we read, "This
was his work, his church" (21). While looking at some fish in the
sea, he wishes, with "an aggrieved note in his voice," that he had a
net with which to catch them to give them to the starving (85). And
he bears the Christian message—in parodied form—to his servant:
"Hell, don't you know that Christ died to save you?" (19). Yet the
Christ that Pierre actually worships is the tangible, material Christ
of monuments and altars—"Christ the Dead, the Beautiful, the
Attenuated!" (22). Selfish, materialistic, ambitious, Pierre admires
and covets the dead body, not the living spirit. The Christ he most
desires is a Rumanian ikon with "its dark heart-shaped head of
Christ, its Mongoloid eyes of pain and charity" (15); to him, it is
more than a work of art—it is a symbol of worldly success.

Because of his selfishness and self-centeredness, Pierre refuses to
become entangled seriously or selflessly with anybody. He is proud
to proclaim that he is an artist and does "not want to be involved"
in either personal or social activities. "Art," he maintains, "knows
no politics; it recognizes no State, and acts, therefore, neither on
behalf of nor against the State. . . . The best policy was to avoid
contact" (109–110). Thus Pierre will not accept the love offered him
by Anna.[4] He believes her unworthy of him and, asking himself
what she could do for him, answers, "Nothing!" (170). To the egoist
that he is, she is merely a strumpet and a whore; and he willingly
accepts her on only a physical basis because he "couldn't live
without having someone to tell about himself" (154). Despite his
personal code of conduct, however, he is at least frank; he is
"honest" with Anna in admitting his inability to love her—a
spiritual, not physical, impotence. His unfair usage of Anna and his
failure to appreciate her are not only his initial misjudgment and
unrealized opportunity to redeem himself; they are also, through
her sister Marthe, the ultimate cause of his death, since Marthe

loathes him and says to Nabil, influencing her lover to shoot him, "He treats [Anna] like dirt and she can't see it. I'd like to cut his throat" (188). (Underlining Pierre's responsibility for his own fate, Newby has him remark just before going out to his death, "I've been wanting to cut my throat" [248].)

Pierre's self-centeredness leads to the bleak condition of noncommunication through isolation. In that state, he becomes incapable of full understanding, either of himself or of others. As Anna reminds him, "there are lots of things" about himself that he does not know (180); and his problem is finally reducible to lack of knowledge, or to imperfect or incomplete knowledge. There is always a wall or a door between him and what he wishes to find, a situation dramatized early in the novel. In his apartment Pierre keeps the "communicating door" between the "central room" and his bedroom "nailed up"; and he goes to much trouble to run two empty rooms into one, "but not by knocking down the wall. That would be too crude" (17, 19). In his relationship with other people, he faces the nailed-up door, the closed-off empty rooms; and in the end he desperately exclaims, "You don't know what a hell my life is" (247).

On his trip to Kole to get away from Anna, Pierre meets a young serving girl called Second Person because she never uses any personal pronoun but the second person singular. This character is identifiable as a complement of Anna, and they serve the same function in the novel. Anna concretely in the city, Second Person allegorically in the mountains—both offer Pierre love and grace, which are theologically synonymous. Of Second Person, Pierre says that "you never saw such grace" (222); and allegorically—for she is encountered against the same allegorical landscape as Pegia—the name is an obvious reference to the Second Person of the Trinity, Christ the Redeemer. Interesting, and thematically important, is the fact that Anna's name means grace. Toward the end of the novel, Pierre turns from Anna to seek Second Person and makes a journey to the mountain café. But, when he arrives there, he finds only a priest, Brother Drosso, from whom he learns that Second Person has died. Of his journey there ("you couldn't say it was an easy road to negotiate"[226]), he thinks: "There was nothing more involved than a journey to a certain point which for certain reasons had turned out to be fruitless" (227). But the journey is not fruitless: the priest is there.

Before Pierre returns to Kole on the journey to find Second Person, "the ideal woman" (222), he has undergone an emotional and spiritual change. This has been caused by his fateful "providential" (134) encounter with the doctor, who foreshadows and contrasts with the priest in the later episode of the novel. Functioning in the "amusing" role of "prophet" (117), Pegia has stressed to Pierre the need for action in life and has issued a call: "We must mobilize. We need a man to awaken the country" (136). Later, Pierre is slowly and almost subconsciously to recognize, erroneously and therefore ironically, this great man in Nabil. (The irony of the doctor as a false prophet is hinted at in the word *mobilize*. He uses Pierre's car not only to carry him away from his work against disease but to carry him to his death, a "fall.")

But, more importantly, Pegia also tells Pierre: "We have to earn the world. . . . A man has to create something to earn the right to live" (136). "To create," he specifies, is "to do something active and positive for human happiness." Pierre accepts this remark as "a personal message for himself," a "watchword" (137). And the words of the physician work on Pierre much as his medicine does on the peasants: "The atabrin so affects the system that the patient himself feels that he is sufficiently fortified to go out into the fields to work, and, as a result, drops dead" (31). In offering his services to Nabil, Pierre thinks he will at last be *doing* something—"Anything, it doesn't matter what. I don't care what [the revolutionaries] want or what they are doing" (248). But he is merely acting unwisely and indiscriminately in a situation which he does not understand. (Anna has tried to inform him about Nabil's real activities; but Pierre, not wanting to be involved, has refused to listen.)

The doctor's words of high sentiment and purposive action "stuck" and "Pierre was to remember them" (136). The circumstance of the doctor's death places Pierre in a position of uneasy prominence since Pierre's own survival is viewed as something of a miracle. Because of his vain sense of self-importance, he is susceptible to such flattering suggestions as that of Soureili, who says to him: "The good God chose you. For some reason the good God chose you [instead of Pegia] to be saved" (151–152). (It is hardly necessary to dwell on the theological double meaning—one not intended, however, by the Pasha—in the words *chose* and *saved*.) Pierre sees his life as having been spared by God because "he was an artist" (157). "What have I done to be saved?" he asks; "Well, to begin with there was that church that I restored." His self-esteem enhanced by such an idea, he tells Anna: "I've been saved for something. . . . I feel that there is a purpose in my life" (158-159).

But, as time passes, Pierre cannot discover this purpose; confused, he "seemed to have given up regular work" and even "all the ordinary pretences of love-making" between him and Anna "were fast disappearing" (204). (It is, surely, important that Pierre never *builds* anything: he only restores and rehabilitates. As an "artist," he fails in creativity; but he does succeed professionally where he cannot privately. His own life remains, despite his efforts, unrehabilitated.) He now begins to wonder whether, in uniting himself with Nabil, he might not serve his own interests by not only "seeing dramatic events taking place" but by obtaining "a few pickings" (206). Then Soureili gives Pierre a new car and, in order to embarrass the present government, sends him to Kole to write a report about the province. So Pierre heads for Kole and reunion with Second Person.

The priest, whom he meets instead, recognizes a spiritual crisis in Pierre, who is "wrestling with himself, bewildered" (231); but the priest perceives that Pierre's condition is not really due only to the news of the serving girl's death. Brother Drosso, attempting to assist Pierre, takes him to the monastery, where he offers him hospitality and audience. Pierre apprehends that the men of the monastery "have a mastery over life," have "little private secrets and comforts that were effective under the most trying conditions," and know how "to overcome the enemy" (233-235). But, while the priest talks to Pierre about the Christian ideal of acceptance and forbearance, Pierre turns against him.

Influenced by the doctor's rousing precepts and by Nabil's example, Pierre has now become an activist and equates action with life. He is harassed by his inability to reconcile the world of the ideal, which has form and meaning, with the real world, which, to him, lacks both (as exemplified in the death of Second Person and in his own confusion) and is pointless. His materialism exerts its power over him, and he says to the priest, "A resurrection is not of the spirit but of the body, the miserable broken bodies" (239). Then, "You are Death" (240), he tells Brother Drosso and declares that he hates him. The circle of Pierre's experience is closing. He has rejected brotherly love and romantic love; now he is to reject divine love and to affirm belief in its opposite: "We have to hate, that is the important thing. Hate. I can at least begin to understand things when I begin to hate" (241). Of course, Pierre does not "begin to understand"; there is, despite the wine they have drunk communionally, no communication between him and Brother Drosso. The Christian teaching is not acceptable to the artist-quester; he is blind to the priest's point. Love can be passive, a witness; it can accept. Hate has to be active, an agent; it must reject. Now Pierre goes down from the mountain, where it is "pleasant" (242), and toward the fate that he has, so ironically, prepared for himself. His descent parallels and balances with Pegia's fall.

To find Pierre's death *thematically* pointless is to misread the novel. The meaning is presented through Newby's paradoxical technique in using negative examples in his plot and by implying affirmative principles with ironic devices. Since the postwar condition rejected an outright positive statement, the artist, to communicate, relies on the skill of indirection. Newby's characters are not sympathetic because they are spiritual failures. The reader is hardly meant to like or to admire them, but he is intended to arrive at a positive statement about spiritual values; about brotherly, romantic, and divine love; and about right action through the characters' failure.

In a later work, a novel written for juveniles, *The Loot Runners* (1949), Newby explicitly states his thematic concern: "It is what's wrong with the world today. When people hear of some bestiality or other they say, 'What's it got to do with us?' and carry on with their own stupid, self-satisfied little existences while others suffer" (53). Here, in *Agents and Witnesses*, we see that action *per se* is non-moral. A life of action not based on a valid ethical system, the novel shows, is not only worthless, so far as intangible and eternal matters are concerned; but it is, finally, destructive. "To what can we compare life?" Pierre has asked the priest and has himself answered, "We can compare life to what it might have been" (241). The ethical norm of the novel, the norm by which to measure what life might be, is clearly Christian love, which is selfless, involving, helping, and ceaseless.

*Agents and Witnesses* is technically a flawed work. It attempts too much in too concentrated a manner in too constricted a structure; and its obsessive preoccupation with theme stultifies characterization. But Newby's having written it in an age lacking in faith is a worthy testimony to his seriousness and to his integrity.

## CHAPTER 3

# England and Wales

IN the period 1948-1951 Newby published four novels: *Mariner Dances* (1948), *The Snow Pasture* (1949), *The Young May Moon* (1950), and *A Season in England* (1951). While enlarging his range and devising new forms, he continued to employ archetypal motifs and patterns as underlayers of plot and as vehicles of theme. The movement of these four narratives, like that of *A Journey to the Interior*, is, in Newby's own phrase, "from misunderstanding to reconciliation"; and their subject is "human relationships" developed through use of "the traditional material of love and 'a-political' adventure."[1] In each of these four novels the human relationships are, in different ways, family relationships; and two of the novels, *The Snow Pasture* and *The Young May Moon*, center around adolescent boys (as do also Newby's two books for juveniles published during this same period, *The Spirit of Jem* and *The Loot Runners*).[2] In all four works, the scene is Britain—England and Wales—and Newby displays in them a rare skill in description and evocation of place, perhaps the finest of its kind in English fiction since D. H. Lawrence.

### I Mariner Dances

Like its predecessor, *Mariner Dances* consists of a double plot. One deals with the adventures and misfortunes of Mariner in his attempts to establish a permanent relationship through marriage with a young girl named Mary. The other plot deals with Fred Paul and his relationship with his family, especially his sister Gladys. A longtime friend of Fred, Mariner intrudes upon the Pauls, first alone and then with Mary, whom he has brought away from her foster parents. Mary falls ill and the Pauls take her into their home. When Mariner finally tells Mary that he already has a wife, Mary and Gladys run away. Fred and Mariner go after them, and at last

Mary agrees to marry Mariner after his divorce, but only on certain strict terms that she dictates herself. Fred and Gladys—through this adventure, which has followed hard upon Fred's unsuccessful attempt to press Keynes, one of his colleagues, into marriage with Gladys—reach a deeper and richer understanding of each other. While Fred attains new knowledge, of self and others, Mariner moves from emotional disorder to order through the imposed discipline and demands of love.

*Mariner Dances* is structured on the classic plot of comedy,[3] a formula which provides clear and strong outlines, as well as a quick pace, that individualize this work among Newby's novels. The lovers, Mariner and Mary, encounter various obstacles to their union, among them the traditional one of parental objection. Mary's guardians believe that Mariner, who is over thirty, is too old for a girl of nineteen. Not only is Mariner without employment and money, but he is also already a husband. The resolution is brought about by a plot twist and a reversal of character. Mary, until now entirely submissive to Mariner, whose "word" was "law" to her (173), abruptly leaves him and refuses to accept him until he orders his way of living and obtains a divorce. The ending, effected by this reversal of roles, is thus happy; and the four principals (Mariner, Mary, Fred, Gladys), after working out the terms of their future relationship, proceed to a dance, one of the festive rituals of comedy.

Mariner and Fred function as the traditional doubles of comedy: both young men are schoolmasters; both are involved in romantic intrigue. Mariner is trying to marry Mary; and Fred, who is not married, is repeatedly urged to marriage by his father but is adamant in postponing the act until he has found a husband for Gladys. "I was taking . . . seriously," he says, "what, by its very nature, was comic—for what was more ludicrous than a man's husband-hunting for his sister . . . ?" (73). Both young men's actions are parallel in being equivalents of rape. Taking Keynes home to meet Gladys, Fred has "all the feelings of having made a raid and carried off some living booty" (84); and Mariner, a "married man in the process of kidnapping an innocent virgin" (64), having already made off with Mary once, declares later that, if she returns to her guardians, "I shall go to that house and drag her out of it by force" (200).

Yet the two men are contrasting opposites as well as doubles. Mariner is passion and foolhardiness; Fred, reason and caution. "No one," Fred remarks, "could give himself so completely over to his passions as Mariner" (149). Mariner is detached from family and place; Fred is strongly attached to both. Mariner, more "humour" than character, undergoes no change or growth of personality; for him to change or develop is impossible. Death, a subject he not infrequently raises in threats or discussions of suicide, is the only alternative to his being and remaining what he is. The solution to his problems is discipline and control, and these have to be imposed from without by another and only through the agency of love.

Mariner is static, but Fred is dynamic and his life is a current running between the poles of school at Handown, where he teaches during the week, and home at Baughton, where he goes for weekends and holidays. A principal irony is that Fred becomes "educated" as a result of the irruption on the scene of Mariner, an "emotional thunderbolt" (14). Mariner "teaches" through the creation of disorder by displacing people, feelings, and attitudes, thus causing them to be viewed or viewable in a new light and from a new angle. Fred lives vicariously and responds to others' activity with quiet envy; Mariner is immersed in life and is restless with activity. Thus, sailing into the novel on the "waves of love" (148), Mariner acts as a life-force that rallies Fred, almost in spite of himself, into action and movement. As Fred notes, ironically unaware of the application to himself, "There was death in inactivity" (17). In this respect, Fred contrasts with his father, who, though under threat of imminent death from a bad heart, defiantly remains an active person.

Although a flat character, Mariner ("What a funny name!" [78]) is superbly realized and is not only the most exciting element in the novel but its outstanding achievement. The art lies not in "developing" him but in revealing what sort of person he is—in convincingly revealing the consistency of his complexity. Newby accomplishes this difficult portrait by two means. First, he shows Mariner in action, and the antics make the man. Fred recognizes, through his sister, that Mariner is "a comic character and his doings absurd. . . . [He] was a pantomime character. There was farce in his victories and in his tragedies only pathos" (116).

Second, Newby brings Mariner into contact with the other major characters and records their reactions to him and their descriptive estimates of him. Consequently, the novel contains a long catalogue of epithets. "Irked" by Mariner's "watery hedonism" (19), Fred sees him as a child and identifies his "humours" quality: "Mariner was not a man: he was a sentiment. He was unhappiness and nothing more" (11). "Imitative as a monkey" (20) and possessing "a hell of a nerve" (139), he seems to Fred "weak and vacillating," "unscrupulous"; but Mariner "could not conceive that he was any other than as he imagined himself" (57). Mr. Paul, who dislikes Mariner but makes him his "main topic of conversation" (116), has a similar view: "There's little good in that man. 'E's weak, weak as water" (79); but later he qualifies this opinion: " 'E's all right, though. Got to put yourself in 'is position" (143).

In time, even Mary can speak realistically, which is harshly, of Mariner; she admits that he is a "cheap liar" and that "there is no sort of responsibility in him" (171). Likewise, brief acquaintance with Mariner is enough for strong and accurate evaluation: "An irresponsible bastard," observes one of his short-term landlords (162). Thematically, Mariner in effect describes himself when he comments on raindrops as "unreasoning things in motion" (12). Weak he is, as the water imagery indicates; but he is also a strong-willed man, and in that trait lies his power. The combination is paradoxically attractive and repellent. The best overall evaluation of him comes from the perceptive Mr. Paul; Mariner, he says, is "the sort of man as'll worry you so much you've just got to get rid of him. Then, when he's gone you want him back" (78).

Fred is the first-person narrator of the novel. As self-portrayer, he not only provides a single, hence unifying, point of view for the work but also, because of his candor and integrity, narrows the emotional distance between story and reader. While he relates what happens during the progress of the narrative, he simultaneously comments on characters and events and charts his own increasing awareness and understanding. He has just resettled after serving in the war and, "glutted with the sense of family" (32), is content to luxuriate in the newly reestablished order and security of the country. "I was feeling surer of myself, more reliant on the obvious evidence of my senses than at any time since I took off my uniform"; "There was organisation, an interconnection of human lives and motives, a beautiful sanity" (30). After a year of this, he says, "one lost the sense of wonder," and he sums up his position by stating, "The retreat from chaos [of war] became less a voyage of discovery" (31). But, ironically, Mariner impresses him and takes him out to sea; on this new voyage of discovery Fred will find that "reality trembles" (169).

He must face up to and deal with two family problems: his father, who is fatally ill; and Gladys, representative of "everything that was broken and beautiful" (127), who is permanently lame as a result of Fred's having as a child accidentally shot her.[4] Primarily through Mariner's advent, Fred comes into a fuller comprehension—and appreciation—of both these members of his family. Fred admits that until now he "had classified my father too glibly" (54). During Fred's wartime absence the men have become strangers and foreigners, intolerant of each other's differences. Yet toward the end, when Mr. Paul has at last been forced to bed, Fred—no longer "glutted"—realizes: "Even as late as this I was learning things about him; no, was beginning to learn a little about him. I was greedy for more" (210). In their final scene together in the novel Mr. Paul offers his commonsensical advice to his son. "I won't 'ave you giving up your own life," he says, "with some daft idea your job is to look after [Gladys]. It'd not be fair to Glad and it'd be not fair to yourself. You just can't let her be a drag on you. What's done is done. You've got your own life to make. . . . You get married. . . . The best way you can serve Glad is to make 'er into an auntie" (211). The effect upon Fred is powerful: "He said good night. . . . I had no wish to leave him there lying in the cool candlelight. But when I did so all the emotion that I had been holding back with my thoughts of stress and struggle, strength and contempt, settled like dew on a summer night." (211).

Fred's psychologically complex relationship with Gladys is one which she as well as their father finds abnormal. Fred has returned from the army to find her, at twenty, surprisingly mature. He attempts to mitigate his morbid sense of guilt and despair about her by being "extra nice and kind" to her (41), but he has actually created instead a situation of falseness, awkwardness, and uncomfortable self-consciousness. Keen and realistic, Gladys accuses him of treating her in "the most disgusting way" (178) and of wanting to dispose of her, through marriage, as a burdensome responsibility. As with his father, Fred comes to comprehend and to acknowledge how little he has really known his sister.

Gladys's situation, no less than Mary's, is viewed by Fred, as narrator, in terms of imprisonment; and the theme of freedom in human relationships becomes the dominant theme of *Mariner Dances*. Each of the principals has something, physical or psychological, that is a bond. Responsible and conscientious, Fred has been long bound by conventional demands—parental, collegiate, military, familial, professional. And there is the sense of guilt about Gladys which he cannot shake off. Gladys is bound to her family by her lameness and is caught in the "coil" and "clutch" of their love (148). Mary is bound to Mariner by his tyrannical will. Mariner is bound to his wife.

It is the young women's act of running away which frees everybody. In response to the "urge for freedom" (197), they strike out for themselves. Thus Gladys proves, particularly to Fred, that she really is capable of making "an independent life in her own right as a human being" (183). She has broken free of the Paul home, which, with the dying father, has come to represent death and sterility to Fred;[5] she has by that act defeated her enemy, pity; and she has freed Fred as well, so that a natural, open, and less exacting relationship can now exist between them. Through flight, Mary puts herself outside Mariner's influence and gains freedom of choice in the matter of living with him. When she agrees to accept him, she stipulates that he must now act with deliberation and decisiveness in divorcing his wife. That he must now, and henceforth, concede and defer to Mary is in no way a loss of freedom but, rather, a paradoxically greater freedom—greater because it is controlled and disciplined, not random and irrational. In the scene that settles all these matters, Newby removes the masks of illusion (self-deceit) from the young men's eyes. One of Newby's favorite themes, appearance and reality, is thus again present along with the theme of imprisonment and freedom.

The entire narrative of *Mariner Dances* acquires wider scope and deeper implications through its symbolism. The two young women's quitting Baughton is an escape to freedom as well as a sport; it is hence an "escapade," as both Fred and Gladys term it (212, 223), in two senses. This theme is reinforced by the symbolism of the seasons. The opening and middle sections of the novel occur

during winter, season of death and inaction, and contain much incidental winter imagery. When the rains and then the floods come,
they suggest and promise rebirth and growth and—in the case of
the rising waters—an overflowing of bounds and barriers. The
ending takes place during the first months of spring:

> Winter was passing, its tension had relaxed and the softness of fertility was
> in the air. Men, tractors and horses were busy in the fields, an old man
> passed . . . with a bundle of sticks for his fire, a swarm of birds left the brown
> tilth when a man in a white hat came out from the shelter of the hedge.
> The fecundating breath of the new season was opening the door of a prison,
> the elvers moved up the rivers, the squirrel appeared, the earth, and the
> rain and the sun conceived. Life stirred in the inert land. Gladys's dis-
> appearance was a process of nature. (197)

The search for the girls gives two additional thematic dimensions
to this cosmic framework. Fred seeks for Gladys at the home of their
aunt, a kind of ironic sibyl who cannot tell the seeker where to go.
Hers is a bizarre, fantastic place with "an air of occult significance," the Gnomes' cottage on the Sugar Plum Common (195).
This is a hybrid world of myth and fairy tale where quests end in
freedom from bondage and physical ugliness (both associated with
Gladys through her crippled leg). This episode, like the season imagery, presages release, reunion, a new beginning, happiness.

Then, in a repetition of the same idea but with a different set of
referents, both Fred and Mariner look for Gladys and Mary in a
town in the Potteries. This brief episode is metaphorically a journey
to the mythical underworld, which has been foreshadowed by the
gnomish, sibylline aunt. In this "sombre" town, "the pottery kilns
squatted in the streets. Smoke drifted along the pavements at face
level. Furnaces roared out of a daylight obscurity, street after street
of flat-faced, expressionless houses ran away under slate roofs
towards final ruin. . . . [There was] a common, marsh almost,
which was littered with the carcases of cast-off omnibuses and street
cars" (202). The reader inevitably infers from this passage that the
young men are reenacting the search for Persephone, with whom
both Mary—who, "in some deep way, seemed a promise of life"
(186) and whose proper "environment" is "the open air"
(170)—and Gladys are identifiable. The theme of freedom from

bondage is again sounded contrapuntally against the action on the literal level.

Newby, given to such fugal treatment of mythical archetypes, further suggests that Mary also brings into the novel strains of the Christian myth. Her name, like so many of Newby's characters',[6] points toward this meaning since she is associated in Fred's narrative with the words *miracle (miraculous), emanation, virgin.* Through her, Fred regains his lost sense of wonder, and Mariner gains a new life—one that replaces his former disordered, meaningless existence. Through love and marriage Mary redeems Mariner, who "idolizes" her (15); and she gives him an ideal to follow and adhere to. The faint suggestion of Christian salvation dovetails with the idea of pagan cyclic rebirth, and the two concepts merge into one.

The novel concludes with another cosmic symbol, the dance—a manifestation of happiness, celebration, union. The dance, a standard symbol of high order and patterned movement, not only brings Mary (who made it "seem important to all of us" [218]) and Mariner together in a state of harmony but serves to indicate the new, civilizing order in Mariner's existence: "Whereas there had been a time when Mariner proceeded by leaps and bounds, dragging Mary after him, he now walked cautiously, respectfully treading in her footsteps" (218). The lovers actually leave the narrative by disappearing into a mass of dancers: "The music presided over the dancers and welded them into one animal, many-smiling, many-talking, many-coloured" (218).

Gladys remarks that what is important to Mary "is not [Mariner] but the dancing" (219). She is stating, Fred notes, a principle of existence—order imposed on activity—and not merely "referring to what was going on at that particular moment." Gladys "can dance a little" herself, she says (220); and the new relationship between her and Fred is consolidated. Fred now can (and does) accept her as she *is*, freely; from now on, they will be not crippler and crippled but brother and sister. "There was," he says, "an urge to call her sister, a word I normally never used in addressing her" (222). Thus the second reconciliation is completed, and all four characters journey forth into the green world of springtime.

Charming as *Mariner Dances* is on the literal level, it makes its fullest statement on a deeper level. The four young people collapse, as thematic archetypes, into two—one man, one woman. Fred and Mariner, reason and passion, combine to make complete Man. Gladys and Mary, closely identifiable by age, situation, mutual understanding and sympathy, and metaphorical function, merge into Woman. Abstractly, they are the eternal feminine which the eternal male seeks; and their union is productive of life, one which nature reflects in the cyclic pattern of the seasons. In a myth-conscious age, Newby's significance as an artist and his importance as an innovator lie in his ability to combine the individual and the archetypal into a seamless whole. The technique also affords him a method—distinctively his own—of scrutinizing man *sub specie aeternitatis*. He has, as yet, not surpassed the brilliant and masterly use of that technique in *Mariner Dances*.

## II   The Snow Pasture

*The Snow Pasture* is an oblique and cryptic work; and most reviewers, perplexed, found it disappointing. George D. Painter, however, in an excellent review, made several extraordinarily perceptive remarks that justified high evaluation of not only this particular novel but Newby's fiction in general. Painter's central point, and one that best serves as an approach to this difficult novel, is that Newby's "novels are so eager and powerful in their story-telling, that we tend to imagine they have plots. Instead, as is frequent in Henry James, they have constructions."[7]

The "construction" of *The Snow Pasture* consists of material, themes, and character-types Newby had already used. The setting, which is symbolic, is a natural reflection of, or parallel to, the dominant mood and situation. In *A Journey to the Interior*, the desert equates with Winter; in *Agents and Witnesses*, mountain and plain stand for the significant and the futile in Pierre's quest for meaning; and, in *The Snow Pasture*, the blackened world of a Welsh mining valley matches the protagonist's emotional condition and stands in contrast with the vital green world of the Cotswolds where his father-in-law lives.

The protagonist, Dr. Robert Pindar, like Fred in *Mariner Dances*, has just returned from war; and he claims that its effects upon him, in the boredom of peace, have affected his work and his relationships with his wife Evelyn and their young son Benjamin. The prime mover of action is Clem Johns, a Welsh working-class boy, Ben's "butty," who functions in the novel like Mariner and is much like him in personality and outrageous behavior. The movement of the narrative—coinciding with the movement of the seasons as in *Mariner Dances*—is from alienation to reconciliation, from a "desolate sense of life to the act of living" (135). This movement through a series of formal patterns constructs the novel. Painter calls *The Snow Pasture* "an exercise in permutations," and the changes of groupings of characters around Clem are precise and symmetrical like the movements and formations of a *corps de ballet*. Missing this aspect of the novel, a reader misses its point and, like one reviewer, tends erroneously to find the construction "flimsy."[8]

The groupings around Clem involve three families—the Pindars, the Hubbards, the Johnses—in and out of which moves Evelyn Pindar's eccentric father, O'Connor. Robert Pindar and Tim Hubbard have bought a medical practice together in Monmouthshire. The Pindars have become estranged and their son is running wild with Clem; and, for these reasons, Evelyn decides to go to her father in Bibury, taking Ben with her. During their absence, Robert takes Clem into the house with him; Clem remains there even after Evelyn and Ben return; and O'Connor soon joins them. These characters make the first grouping in the novel, and O'Connor's actions lay the groundwork for the two later groupings. He takes an instant fancy to Clem and arranges with the boy's family for him to remain permanently with the Pindars. O'Connor also takes an instant liking to Tim because of their mutual interest in gambling.

"Bright and eager about life" (56), Clem has a profound and unsettling effect upon the Pindars. He is a "novelty" (108), and his presence gradually leads them to examine their motives and their behavior. A real bond between husband and wife develops—but it is a stronger one than that between them as father and mother to Ben. Robert's attachment to Clem becomes so marked as to cause gossip; and Evelyn, whom the boy holds in almost reverential awe, responds to him so utterly that he comes close to displacing her own son in her affection.

The second grouping occurs after Evelyn makes a second trip to Bibury. Having returned to his own home, her father became seriously ill and has died. To the surprise and consternation of Robert and Evelyn, O'Connor has left all his money to Clem and has named Tim as trustee. Clem now goes to live with Tim and

Erica Hubbard, but he wants to return to the Pindars. Ben determines that he shall be taken back, but Robert and Evelyn refuse. Erica gives birth to a son, and shortly afterward the Pindars go to Bibury. This trip signals the third grouping.

During the Pindars' absence, Clem acts strangely; he attempts to shoot his father, then himself. Consequently, Tim says that he must give up Clem and the trusteeship. Upon returning to Wales, Robert decides that both Clem and his inheritance must be placed where they belong—with Clem's own parents. When Robert effects this arrangement, Clem is back where he began; the pattern has come full circle. Meanwhile, Robert and Evelyn have recovered their lost intimacy and have put their relationship with their own son back on the proper, "natural" footing. The novel ends with the disclosure that Evelyn is to have another child.

Such a simplification as this, while it reveals the structural outline of the narrative, obviously distorts the fluid rhythm of the subtle emotional and psychological relationships among the characters. While it plots the steps, it omits the gestures, stances, and experiences of the dancers. But it adequately indicates what happens and how structure and events—the three groupings around Clem, the three trips to Bibury, and the advance of the seasons—comprise a unified, intelligible action. The question of meaning now arises.

The alert reader is immediately aware of the beginning of a system of incremental imagery announced by the word *snow* in the title of the novel. On the second page of the text he encounters *frozen* and *cold*, and they are readily identifiable as thematic. Evelyn says to Robert: "You don't feel any more. You're hard, frozen, dead! You've no guts. Somebody else has been doing the thinking for you the last few years and your brain's gone cold" (8). The narrative movement of alienation to reconciliation is the harmonic accompaniment to the theme of the novel—indifference. This negative state, productive of alienation and isolation, must yield, or change, to its opposite—feeling, concern—which then produces reconciliation and union. Proverbially, indifference is, metaphorically, coldness. Thus theme and imagery are joined and shape the meaning of the novel.

As the narrative moves through its ever more psychologically complex groupings, the "cold" imagery continually recurs; it all culminates and climaxes in a passage near the end dealing with "snow-meadow" and "snow pasture." The imagery has come to represent not only an emotional condition (coldness) but its inevitable consequence (alienation, loneliness), as Robert finds in his own experience. Such a condition is "unnatural" (an epithet that is also recurrent in the narrative), just as the title suggests through its paradoxical superimposition of a death-isolation symbol, snow, upon a life-crowd symbol—pasture, grasslands for grazing. Snow is of course "natural," but its presence in meadows or pastures renders them temporarily unable to fulfill their purpose—that is, unnatural. The cyclic return of warm weather and the increased heat of the sun remove the snow and restore the meadow to its natural function: the grass grows; the flocks or herds appear. As spring and summer encroach in the background of the novel, there is promise that this more "natural" situation is to occur in the foreground also. The metaphor of the pasture is a cosmic parallel to Robert.

Robert himself is metaphorically snow-covered. He has been frozen by the death of his brother, who is very much like Ben: "I loved him more than almost anything else in the world. And when he was killed in the war I found myself *hating him*. . . . Why? Because I loved him so much. When he died I thought he had played some dirty trick upon me . . . , I felt that he had deserted me, hurt me in some deliberate way. I was hurt so much that I think I must have said to myself, 'I'm not going to let anybody or anything hurt me again' " (27). Robert retains a vivid memory, "the memory of his brother and himself, as they had been, the pair of them, racing across the frozen meadows, years before, at the beginning of the world" (28).

But Robert blames the war itself for his present lethargic condition: "It hasn't left me whole. I want to draw into myself, find my own protection. I can't love Eve and Benjamin as much as I should. I can't give them enough of myself" (62). But the narrator, reversing the cliché of the psychological war wound, corrects this idea: "He [Robert] was deceiving even himself. . . . Robert had invented his own loneliness, not the war" (62). He is afraid of life, a man without "guts" (a repeated charge against him); hence, he has withdrawn to the isolated mining valley, away from the green world of the Midlands. He becomes a "passive watcher" (214) and is like the doctor in *Agents and Witnesses:* he cannot heal himself.

The visionary memory of the brother is balanced toward the end of the novel by another vision, the occasion of the title. This second vision is a reversal of an earlier scene in which Robert saw Ben, "ruddy in the sunshine" (119), going off to play. He yearned for communion with his son and would have liked to shout to him to come back. But he hesitated, out of fear, and the moment with its opportunity passed. In the repetition, Robert responds to the offering of the moment—responds emotionally and imaginatively:

Robert stood and watched [Ben and Clem]. They were at the end of the glade and, as they turned to make for the gate in the wall, Benjamin looked back and his face was dim and remote in the half-light. He looked back and waved his arm as, once before, he had looked back on the glassy mountainside before making off through the bracken to climb once more the slope with his toboggan. But on this occasion Robert did not want to call him back. The "Come back, come back" had been the instinctive utterance of a lonely man, lonely in spite of his wife and his child and his work. And now, for the first time, this same summons came for him. From that high, cold altitude where Robert too had wandered, the boy Clem was calling for his aid. He heard the miner's son cry from the icy solitude. By those frosts and those gales Robert had been tired utterly. Why should a child climb where a man had been shaken, and why did pity wait so long? The trial was too much for man or child and Robert's body responded with a dry, bitter, tearless weeping.

There was a break in the trees and he could see the last of that day's sun resting on the far side of the valley. In a cottage garden the white nets that had been cast over the currant bushes shone like heaps of snow.

If he could have spoken it would have been to himself, "Go back, go back." He had walked alone and climbed high enough. The sunlight lengthened and more and yet more of the currant bushes could be seen in cottage garden after cottage garden, a cold drift of purity under an empty sky, a window into the chill pasture of snow-fields lying in visionary remoteness; and here Clem stood and sent his call.

"Benjamin," Robert suddenly shouted. (190)

The clue to this passage lies in an earlier one:

She [Evelyn] had noticed a greater warmth in Robert's nature, a relaxation of tenseness, a greater softness, a deference to the claims and privileges of her own feminine nature, since Clem had come to live with them. The boy had achieved something which their own son never had the power to do: the promise . . . that the resistance in Robert's heart might break down, the look of distance be taken out of his eyes, that they might abandon the larger and desolate sense of life to the act of living. Benjamin O'Connor [her father] . . . had had some appreciation of this. He had seen how Clem was a point of radiance from which a larger glow might—without the boy's knowing how he had been made use of—in time extend. (135)

Clem, then, is metaphorically the sun, the youthful agent in the narrative who brings or bestows light, warmth, life, energy. He melts the coldness in Robert, who has become "dead and cut off out of the sun" (125); and Robert's feeling for him is "the first pathetic flowering of the arid loneliness of his spirit" (70). Through his acts, Clem first awakens and then redirects Robert's feeling; therefore, Clem is responsible both for the eventual reconciliation of the Pindars with each other and with their son and for the coming of another child in their family. Thus another pattern emerges in the groupings: Tim has a son; both Robert and Johns recover their sons; and, not only to symbolize the reconciliation and the future but also to indicate the periodic, cyclic aspect of nature, Robert will obtain another child of his own. At the end, Robert and Evelyn—called Eve, the archetypal mother—are become "one flesh" (224), a condition of wholeness their new child will embody. In a scene of pure ritual, Robert says to Evelyn: "You're like a high-priestess of some mysterious cult receiving a would-be initiate" (223). Their new intimacy "marks a new beginning" (224).

Slowly reanimated, Robert is now whole again; internal feeling and external act coincide and are in harmonious correspondence—with each other and with nature. "Feeling," Robert acknowledges, "had to be fought with an intenser feeling" (214). Quotidian life is not a state of peace, boredom, and indifference; such life is itself a kind of war in which preservation calls for affirmative action, not passive watching (as Pierre Bartas also learned). "Protection lay in action and giving and working and forgetfulness—and where better place for all these than the valley here before him?" (214). This recognition—yet another circling pattern—frees Robert; and the change in metaphor from inactive snow to active water, a change due to solar powers, reinforces the change in the man. "He walked on up the hill, walking into his thankfulness as into a great wave" (214).

III   The Young May Moon

In *The Young May Moon*, Newby again examines experience
from the double angle of adolescent and adult; he also employs
again enriching patterns and motifs from myth and fairy tale. The
work begins not with a marshaling but with a dispersing of characters. Following the unexpected death of his wife Freda, Alec Rice
sends his fifteen-year-old son Philip away from their home in Zion
Terrace to live with relatives in Wales, where the boy is to learn the
baker's trade from his Uncle Adrian. Rice then leaves home himself.
After this introductory action, the novel traces the separate adventures of father and son in alternate chapters until the two come
together again at the end. Narrative movement from separation and
psychological alienation to reunion and reconciliation thus
organically shapes and controls structure.

The stories of father and son are both about obtaining
knowledge. Philip's is, in addition, about growing up and descrying,
through cruelty, the existence of evil, not only outward but inward:
his is thus a story of the "collision of innocence and experience"
which, Newby has written, "most of us never cease to be involved
in, though with diminishing violence, for the whole length of our
lives."[9] Disquieted by the sudden death of his mother, Philip is ad-
ditionally bewildered when his Aunt Bess reveals to him that Freda
was actually his stepmother; his real mother, Laura, he learns, had
left his father and himself when Philip was a baby. She now lives
nearby in Wales; and, though Philip never expresses either interest
in or concern about Laura, Uncle Adrian promises to take him to
see her sometime. "Far from home, in a strange country with
strange people" (47), the sensitive boy succumbs to feelings of
aloneness, abandonment, and betrayal by his father. He tries to
reach him by letter and by telegram, but his efforts are unsuccessful.

Mystified, Philip returns to Zion Terrace to see what he can discover about his father; but the house is deserted. He finds a smashed photograph of Freda fallen onto the floor and his letter to Rice,
unopened. In this letter the boy had written that the news about
Rice's having been left by Laura made not the slightest difference
and that he loved his father as much as ever. Philip now believes,
however, that Rice not only does not know what his son thinks

about him but possibly does not even care. Bitter toward his father, he sees himself "friendless and alone, struggling against a hostile world" (183).

The chapters devoted to Rice create both parallels and an ironic counterpoint to those chapters devoted to Philip. Freda had been a domestic tyrant. After giving her an indecently cheap funeral, Rice reacts to her death with joyousness. Subconsciously, however, he feels guilty; and he tries to purchase back that feeling with a display of sardonic insouciance meant to startle: he tells neighbors and strangers alike that he poisoned Freda. He also feels loveless, like his son; moreover, he is frightened by his widower's liberty because it will place on him the responsibilities which Freda had carried and because it will culminate in loneliness. The situation is intolerable, and he does not know how to cope with it. Consequently, shortly after Philip's departure from Zion Terrace, Rice impetuously leaves on an "unpremeditated flight" (88) to recover from the shock of Freda's death. He flees, like a conscience-burdened wanderer of myth, a self-dubbed "fugitive from justice" (103).

Ironically, while the son is having to contend with the real "world of fact, of pain and anxiety" (154), the father retreats into a pastoral "world of illusion," a fairy-tale world of childhood (155). Happy-go-lucky, he arrives at a secluded inn where he takes lodgings. "Sort of cut off from the world" (107), it is a place of "fantasy" and "enchantment" (155, 154), with a splashing brook, plum trees laden with ripe fruit yellow as honey, and singing nightingales. The inn, once a highwayman's hideout, is kept by a bedraggled woman whose husband stokes at the gasworks. A hateful wicked fairy-tale couple, they mistreat the woman's unwelcome sister, Doll, a sensual barmaid who has just returned from Germany to live with them. An ancient dwarfish man named Elf Griffin frequents the inn for beer. Rice makes love to Doll; but the companionable Griffin warns him that evil will betide him if he remains long in the place. But it is idyllic and Rice, falling under its spell, forgets death and his son. Yet here in this place of withdrawal Rice is eventually to discover and face truths that will fortify him to return to the world of realities. His flight has become a journey to the interior of self, and the mythic pattern of appearance-disappearance-reappearance clearly emerges from the narrative.

A parallel to Rice's escapade in the enchanted forest follows when

Philip goes one Sunday for a swim in the huge reservoir near his relatives' home. His aunt has told him that a drowned village lies beneath the water, and Philip believes that the bells he hears ringing might possibly be those of the submerged church. Pursuing the idea, he achieves tremendous new knowledge:

Since Philip had first heard of the drowned village he had discovered that the possibilities of life were stranger and more terrifying than he had imagined. If hard things like the death of his mother and the disappearance of his father could happen in his own life, why was it impossible to believe that harder things happened in the lives of other people? . . . How it would be at all possible for a village to be overwhelmed in the manner described by Aunt Bess he was unable to imagine. Reason told him that the dam had taken a long time to build and the villagers would have had ample warning . . . of their danger. But he saw too clearly the possibility of such a disaster to doubt that Evil would have means of bringing it about. When he had arrived at Zion Terrace to find that his father had gone, Philip had felt wickedly abandoned. But he now experienced a more searing sense of abandonment, for he had discovered in his own mind the seeds of such malignancy that he feared he might not be as other people were. He was in great agony of spirit. He saw . . . himself in the role of builder of dams and plotting the destruction of little communities. . . . The truly damnable moment came when the plan did not seem insane but as quietly sensible as the baking of a batch of bread. He had not dreamed there was such spiritual suffering as this he now went through. (200-202)

Pressing on "to some icy region of despair" (203), Philip goes to the control tower of the dam and is about to throw the switch of the floodgates when he is interrupted by a shouting man whom he takes to be the devil incarnate. No apparition, the man is Grainger, who is in charge of the pumping station, and it was he, Philip learns, whom his mother Laura had run away with and married. Philip has such an extraordinary resemblance to Laura—a resemblance already commented upon by others—that Grainger has identified him at once as her child. Laura, however, has now been dead two years. This news should have moved Philip, the boy later thinks, but it did not. Yet, of course, it has affected him; and it causes his imagination to run away with him.

He elaborates a fantastic version of his experience at the reservoir. He says that while swimming he dived down and saw the drowned village. When he then went to the dam and emptied the reservoir, the village came back to life. But he let the water in again, redrowning the village. Obviously this episode symbolizes the psychological problem of the boy. His naked swim in the reservoir is a plunge into the imaginative fears of the unconscious. He sees an identity with the drowned, and the dam is an emblem of frustration, restraint, and death. He admits readily that this tale is a lie, but for him it is a manifestation of the evil, and the potential for exercising it, which he has discovered in himself. He thinks: "Why, oh why should there be so much cruelty in the world? Why should he have so much of it within himself? And why should his father reveal . . . that even he had been given his wicked share?" (253). To himself, Philip is "a monster and an outcast from society" (254). Yet out of this terrible discovery and this distressful encounter with evil, love and maturity will develop.

Grainger, once disrupter of union, now becomes the agent of reunion, for, anxious about Philip, he finds Rice and indicates to him his duty to his son. Doll, who is capable of imaginative identification with Philip because she knows what being unwanted feels like, has already challenged Rice on this matter; she has accused him of having shirked his parental duty, through fear, by abandoning Philip and sending him to relatives to learn about Freda's true identity as his stepmother. Rice has admitted the fear—that Philip will go to see Laura, will respond to her with love, and will become contemptuous of the father who was unable to hold her. Moreover, called to duty by Grainger, incited by Doll, and also motivated by the self-critical, disgusting realization that he has lacked imagination, that "great instrument of moral good," Rice at last begins to understand his son's unhappiness and decides to go to him, thus assuming the responsibility he has until now evaded and delegated. Laura's death, news of which Grainger also brings him, removes Rice's fear; but it is to his credit that this news has followed, not preceded, this decision to return.

After Rice's arrival in Wales, atonement of father and son occurs on the side of a mountain, a symbol of their new communion and well-being. The mountain also represents the spiritual height that contrasts and balances with the emotional depth of the episodes in the forest and in the water—symbols of loss, fear, and frustration—where both have made important self-discoveries. During this scene of reunion, the father has finally reached the point at

54 P. H. NEWBY

which he himself must speak to the son about Laura. He tells him a
story from the past.

When Philip was teething, Rice (as he relates) took him outdoors
one night into the cool open air to comfort the crying child and to
let Laura get some sleep. It was a still night in May; the new foliage
and blossoms gave the air a fresh smell; and the moon was but a few
days old. Philip fell quiet in his pram, and Rice too went to sleep.
When he awakened near dawn and heard somebody crying, he discovered it was not the baby but Laura. She was leaning over the
pram, her black hair hanging loosely about her face and down to
her shoulders. Rice pretended to be still asleep; and, when he next
looked up, Laura was gone. That was, he then tells Philip, the day
she left them. Rice's account is "no ordinary anecdote," and the
true and painful moment of its telling is "the hidden, undisturbed
foundation" of Rice's and Philip's "understanding for each other"
(280).

Facing Philip, Rice obtains insight into his own acts and realizes
his folly: the boy's responsive manner discredits the father's long-
held supposition (and fear) that he and Laura were rivals for
Philip's esteem. And Philip, yearning for affection, has restored to
him by his father's return the "capacity to love" (280). His
resemblance to his mother, Philip has thought, had caused Rice to
hate him; but he now sees that the father's love for Laura was
equally love for him.

The absence of the father, therefore, has tested the son; the
return of the father has forced the son "into other ways of feeling
than bitterness and despair"; and "the boy had matured" (313).
Philip "now had a deeper understanding of his father than had ever
previously been possible," and "this understanding had brought
sympathy and a deeper love than a child could ever feel" (317). The
ending of the novel thus fulfills an early observation that it "was in
grief that knowledge lay" (49). Against a setting symbolically reflecting the action, "a landscape from fairyland" (283), where all
tales come to a happy conclusion, father and son go down the
mountainside and cross the dam, over which arches a rainbow, a
multifaceted symbol of union: "Their pleasure in the fleeting rainbow was the first they had knowingly shared that day and it
brought them together as had nothing else. They stood side by side
in the presence of unexpected beauty, and although neither of them

made any comment it had sparked into being such an intimacy that the colours seemed to hang about them as they walked" (282).

The title of *The Young May Moon* indicates through its traditional association with romance that the novel is preeminently a love story. Specifically, it combines two love stories, that of husband and wife and that of father and son. If viewed as a discrete segment, the story of Rice and Laura ends unhappily; but its ending in context—ironic in that Rice, attractive to all women, cannot keep the only woman he really loved—is poignantly modified and mollified by the happy resolution of the story of filial and paternal love which follows and grows from it.

Laura and Rice are both romantic idealizations; and both, by means of the moon, transcend to a supermundane level. Her name itself—Laura—echoes the whole Petrarchan tradition; and Rice, with his faithful love for Laura and his idealized masculinity (convincingly depicted and conveyed both by description and by Rice's effects on various types of women), fits well into that love-centered tradition. Laura's beauty, like Rice's, is repeatedly mentioned; and it serves as the subject of the touching line, spoken by Rice to Philip, that ends the novel—"Please remember . . . that she was beautiful."

Furthermore, Laura's remarkable, superlative beauty helps to establish her as a goddess and as pure femininity; she equates with the moon by being a metaphorical personification of it. (In Thomas Moore's lyric "The Young May Moon," which is undoubtedly echoed in Newby's title, the lady is warned to shun the "Sage's glass" lest "in watching the flight / Of bodies of light, / He might happen to take thee for one.") And balancing with Laura as moon and as female principle, Rice is, by the metaphorical implication that arises from plot and description, not only the male principle but the sun, as evidenced by his warm and open nature, his golden hair, his virility, sensuality, and constancy.[10]

On the deepest level, then, these features of *The Young May Moon* disclose forcefully that it is about cosmic forces symbolized in sun and moon—male and female, life and death. The masculine—father and son, actually one[11]—seeks the feminine and, both through it and in it, finds complementary union and fulfillment. Such is the abstracted story of Rice and Philip. The link that first connected them was Laura; and, after their alienation, it is through her that that connection is reestablished.

This connection, however, could not be made without the resolution of the misunderstandings and the acquisition of knowledge. And the moon of the title is thematically relevant on another level. As a source of light, illuminating darkness, it represents the understanding. This function of the moon is supported by the ancillary imagery system of eyes, the organ of sight and insight productive of knowledge. Details about characters' eyes—a conspicuous characteristic of the Petrarchan tradition—are unavoidably noticeable in the novel; and they serve to indicate, and to emphasize, the subtheme of knowledge and understanding upon which rests the main theme of alienation and reconciliation. In a passage that exposes the moon as a symbolic vehicle of the motifs of both love and understanding, Newby writes of Philip: "He had always . . . had this love for his father. Only for a time it had been obscured by the passing of a cloud; and then it had sailed out, moonlike, into a clear sky, drawing behind it unsuspected tides of understanding" (313). The relationship between love and understanding, the novel thus shows, is symbiotic when that relationship is benignly and properly balanced.

The moon, finally, by being in May and by being young, gives promise of growth and life; it dominates the novel, as does Laura herself, and functions as a unifying device. Growth and life, along with such a lesser narrative symbol as bread, are the opposite of death. In finding and reclaiming each other through love—which is beautiful—both Rice and Philip triumph over death and the effects of death. In this novel, fairy-tale structure proclaims a continuing life of happiness, but Newby avoids falsity and sentimentality by depicting Philip's awareness of the demands of the world of facts and his response to them. The boy wants to be with his father, but acknowledges that he must grant him his own freedom. And Philip, while continuing for a time to learn to bake bread, is planning to become the sort of engineer who builds dams—an irony that dilutes sweetness with the tangy recognition of the quirks and moral ambiguities of human nature.

Warm and humanly wise, *The Young May Moon* is one of Newby's finest novels. It is noteworthy for its characterization; the people are well-rounded creations, sympathetic and memorable. The visual imagination, too, is especially powerful and effective; places as well as persons are all strikingly realized. And the coalescence of literal acts and symbolic patterns is wholly successful, thereby surpassing altogether the craft of *The Snow Pasture*. As Antonia White noticed in her review of this work, nowhere in it has Newby "taken his eye off the mark or slurred or blurred an effect."[12] *The Young May Moon* does more than stand up steadfastly to rereading; it intriguingly draws the reader back.

## IV   A Season in England

In *A Season in England*, Newby turns from the strong affirmative ending of the three preceding novels and of *A Journey to the Interior* to an ambivalent conclusion that leaves his protagonist, Tom Passmore, pursuing a life-in-death existence. Like D. H. Lawrence, though with more discreet techniques that obviate direct authorial comment, Newby conveys unequivocally his own attitude toward his principal characters. Winter, Fred and Mariner, Pindar, Rice and Philip he admires and likes; and his attitude, inevitably, influences the reader's own evaluative attitude toward these characters. *The Snow Pasture* is only partially successful, largely because of Newby's failure to induce the reader's whole sympathy for Pindar, a failure due to narrative assertion of admiration without any displayed justification of it. Just as clearly, Newby dislikes and disrespects Bartas of *Agents and Witnesses*, and he dismisses him, finally, with an abrupt death. Though treated more compassionately and handled with a gentle humor, Passmore also lacks his creator's unqualified admiration and regard; and *A Season in England* progresses inexorably to the disclosure of that fact.

With numerous devices of irony, the novel develops the theme of self-knowledge and introduces a variety of changes in Newby's narrative formulas of misunderstanding-understanding and alienation-reconciliation. Passmore, a lecturer at the state university in Cairo, is going back to England in the summer of 1945 on a holiday which he will turn into a "Mission." One of his English colleagues, Guy Nash, has died a few months earlier; and Guy's Greek widow, Renee, has just refused Passmore's proposal of marriage. Guy had never told his parents, whom he represented as monsters, about his marriage to Renee; and Passmore intends, for a variety of reasons, to tell them about it himself: to do so is his mission.

He visits the elderly Nashes at Whiteleaf, their home in the country. He finds them hospitable, but they are also eccentric and contradictory. Their existence is staidly ritualistic, and they are self-
assured survivors of the Edwardian age. Passmore becomes so fond
of them and they of him, seemingly, that they invite him to stay
with them as long as he likes. Finally, he decides not to tell them
about Renee. Then, unannounced and unexpected, she herself
arrives at Whiteleaf. After an unsettling series of events, the Nashes
accept her into their home. Passmore renews his suit, but Renee
again rejects him.

Meanwhile, she and Mrs. Nash have become very close; and,
when Mrs. Nash falls ill, Renee nurses her attentively. One day the
housekeeper finds Renee in a coma: she has been poisoned.
Passmore discovers that the culprit was Mrs. Clegg, the jealous wife
of the handsome and virile farm manager whom she believes to
have been seduced by Renee. Mrs. Nash, however, admits that she
herself had prompted the woman to poison Renee. Not aware of the
facts, Renee believes that Passmore poisoned her out of passion and
jealousy of her behavior with Clegg; consequently, she is for the
first time attracted to him. When Mrs. Nash, now perhaps fatally ill,
urges Passmore and Renee to go away together and even gives them
a thousand pounds to do so, Renee readily agrees.

They go to London, and Renee expects Passmore to make love to
her; instead, shocked by her sensuality and by what he considers
her cruelty, he lectures her about morality. She leaves the next
morning for the country to care for Mrs. Nash; and Passmore,
after arranging to make a final visit to Whiteleaf, will return to
Egypt, alone.

Technically as well as thematically this material is deeply indebted to Henry James. Extremely well knit, *A Season in England*
displays a remarkable intensity that results from the restriction of
setting, since almost all of the action occurs at Whiteleaf. A more
important cause of intensity, however, is the rigorous use of the
Jamesian central intelligence as the point of view. The entire novel
is conveyed through Passmore, and the reader's knowledge is limited and bounded solely by this character's knowledge. This Jamesian point of view reveals Passmore's mind as a theater of psychological and moral questions, probes, discoveries, and reversals.
Going to England on an apparently simple mission, Passmore finds

himself in an ever-shifting situation of complexities filled with typical Jamesian ironies. Few things are what they seem; doors open upon doors; stark simplicity evolves into polychromatic intricacies.

The following passage displays this Jamesian method. Drawn into an emotional vortex at Whiteleaf, Passmore decides he must escape from the Nashes:

But when and how was he to leave Whiteleaf? Without quite understanding how it had happened, his relationship with the Nashes, which had begun with ordinary kindliness on the one side and respect on the other, was not peculiarly charged with emotion. He had come to Whiteleaf with the intention of telling them about Renee, they had taken his visit to be one of courtesy but how differently everything had turned out! When he left he knew that it would only be, at some future time, to come back—and why not? he thought, why not, in spite of the distressing thought that the kind of relationship he was enjoying with the Nashes would have been almost impossible had Guy been still alive? He was a usurper. Possibly the regard that Mrs. Nash seemed to have for him was built up on nothing more sensible than a chance similarity to Guy; but even so, whom could it harm if she were allowed to persist in her kindness and if he went on with an encroachment which might eventually lead to his playing that part in their lives which Guy had failed to do? (94–95)

Deriving from James, too, are the clash and contrast of English and Eastern nationalities. Passmore frequently contrasts England and Egypt on numerous points; for "having judged England through Egyptian eyes he now thought of Egypt with an English mind" (13). One of the contrasts he makes contributes importantly to an understanding of his moral dilemma because it establishes the basic difference between English and Eastern attitudes and behavior, which are identified through nature. The rain-soaked English countryside, with half-lights and hints, speaks "in a language of curious ambiguity"; in Egypt, "the sun [makes] statements in hard black and white" (130). Sensual, instinctive, and forthright, Renee neither is acquainted with nor understands the manners, customs, and traditions to which she so suddenly introduces herself; and she frequently makes comparisons that are unflattering to the English: "Oh, you English are the true sensualists, with your discipline and your duty and your rules and your

regulations and your sense of sin. Above all your sense of sin. That's
something I've discovered in this house [Whiteleaf]. There's sin in
this house. For me it's a new experience and I wouldn't have missed
it for worlds. It was worth coming all this way to learn that. I
know very well now why Guy didn't want to come home. Puri-
tanism! My God, what a sauce to the feast!" (211).

Renee's presence in England is brought about, moreover, by a
matter common in James's novels—money. Totally without resour-
ces, she comes seeking an income from Guy's parents. Passmore
puts this matter of money into the framework of contrasting
nationalities when he denies that Renee is mercenary: "It isn't as
though you'd turned up and said, 'Look here, give me a thousand
pounds,' and then cleared out of the house immediately. Is it?" To
which Renee, "openly amused," replies, "Oh, you English! That is
precisely what I intended to do" (153).

Finally, Newby's theme itself is Jamesian in essence. The central
subject of A Season in England is the attenuated life—the life not
lived to the fullest and thus wasted; it is a Newbian version of The
Ambassadors. "Live!" advises Strether; and Passmore, though half
in love with death, would "live" if he could. His interest to the
reader is his quest for life and a way of life. He comes to England on
a Liberty ship and, deluded by languorous indiscrimination, looks
for life at Whiteleaf, a place—its very name suggestive of
death—where there is, as Renee exclaims, no air; being there is
"like living in a tomb" (154).

Newby develops Passmore's quest for life on two planes of
narrative movement from misunderstanding to understanding. The
first concerns the family matter of the Nashes, their dead son, and
his wife. Passmore's coming and Renee's, after a series of mazy and
melodramatic events, force revelation and acceptance of truth upon
the family: "We are shown to ourselves for what we are," says Mr.
Nash (254). He and his wife finally understand, acknowledge, and
accept their failure as Guy's parents: "With all good intentions in
the world we failed in the one thing where we wanted to succeed.
Guy leaves us nothing but a sense of—of futility, and wrong-doing,
and—and lack of imagination" (252). Their possessive relationship
with Guy had ironically driven him away and caused him to make a
life independent of, and kept secret from, them. (Hence their ignorance of his marriage to Renee.) As a consequence of this un-

derstanding, they are ultimately prepared to accept Renee and to allow her to live her own life freely—to give her the freedom denied to Guy. Thus alienation of the dead man is replaced by conciliation with the living woman; and thus, as Renee suggests, "poison in small quantities is a tonic" (268).

The second movement from misunderstanding to understanding concerns Passmore's journey from self-ignorance to self-knowledge. This journey branches off from the originating life-quest, runs parallel to it, then rejoins it. All is trenchantly ironic. Passmore is the teacher who, not understanding, must learn; he is the man who is a child, as almost all of the other characters term him in one fashion or another; he is the seeker who gives up what he finds; and he is the reconciler who is left alone. His quest for life is at first unconscious—he does not originally articulate the real reason for going to England; when he consciously recognizes what he is about, he is forced by his weakness to quit his goal and return to where he came from. He is, therefore, the hero failed; he does not return from his grand adventure fulfilled or capable of regenerative actions (having undergone but a negative response to his self-discovery). In the end, he can only count himself "fortunate" (304) for the season in England.

Passmore is *un homme manqué* as well as *un héros manqué*. He enjoys the feeling of irresponsibility: he lives away from his homeland, has lost touch with the people and the country, does not know homesickness, and has no family ties. And he had, moreover, no roots as a child because his family was always on the move. His name itself, Passmore, is implicative of impermanence and restlessness. But he is not one to fail in his duty; serious, intent, and solemn, he dislikes complacency and believes in facing facts. And he thinks himself passionate. About himself he is, ironically, benighted. His holiday in England becomes an excursion into a conflict of opposites: life-death, West-East, England-Egypt, green farms-desert lands, morality-instinct, youth-age. The irony here demonstrates that, while naturally belonging to the one side, Passmore remains on the other.

His lack of wholeness is indicated by his being Guy's double, a fact stressed by his given name, Tom, which means "twin." Passmore and Guy, both Englishmen, follow the same profession in Egypt; they look alike; they have something of the same manner;

they were both even late-born. When Guy dies, Passmore tries to marry his wife—an attempt, still unconscious at that point, to unify himself by taking his double's place. At Whiteleaf, he is at first embarrassed by his doubleness—"I've never been a *doppelgänger* before," he says (57)—but he gradually becomes consciously aware of his drive to wholeness; and he seeks with an "emotional thirst" (63) to complement his self by taking Guy's place in the family. Thus Passmore would acquire all those qualities he has lacked: "a home, a sense of continuity with the past, dignity" (63). The high summer enchants Passmore, and he sees that his happiness in Egypt has been false:

For him at least it was impossible to live with honest contentment in any other country but England. It was obvious that much that was absurd in the English temperament found expression in the two Nashes but Passmore felt at home with this absurdity; it was a statement, over-emphatic perhaps but not distorted, of those particular values which he held himself: conservative values, the dignity of the individual, the belief in a certain austere moral code, a perpetual playing down of the life of passion and an exaltation of common sense, the slightly melancholy charm of maintaining a perhaps outworn tradition. It could all be summed up in the word "home." The Nashes had shown him that a "home" lives in time as well as place. There is, and must be, some sense (even if it is only delusion) of the continuity in the word, and continuity with the past was in the very "feel" of the Nashes and their Whiteleaf. . . . Why could he not belong there? (84–85)

Soon Passmore assumes openly the role of son, and he views the situation metaphorically and romantically. He undergoes a "kind of baptism" in a "flood of sparkling sensation" (186). (Earlier Mr. Nash has said to him that he is "a babe in arms" and does not know he is born yet [65].) As a result, Passmore thinks (ironically) that his sympathies have become enlarged and that his egoism has been lost; he will be reborn as "the ideal son: not Guy, but as Guy should have been" (187). The rebirth leads ironically to a loss of his sense of identity; when Mrs. Nash in delirium thinks him actually to be Guy, Passmore humors her: he pretends that he is the living Guy. Then, by a superb irony, Mrs. Nash assigns a new role to Passmore that ends his present role in the drama at Whiteleaf: freedom. Passmore-as-Guy must accept the freedom the Nashes had failed to give their son in life so that they, as parents, can feel they have now vicariously corrected their failure and made an act of penance through belated compensation. Thus Passmore as himself has no place at Whiteleaf; he as Guy has been let loose.

When he realizes in London that Renee too will never accept him, Passmore has reached the end of possibilities. She has once told him that he is "not a man" but a "stick of wood" (212); now she stigmatizes him as "slow—and a little dull" (288). She wants "to see some life" (289). The moment of truth now arrives for Passmore on his journey to self-knowledge: "Life, he thought, how much of it he had been missing" (289). At this point, the divergent quests for self-knowledge and for life have now reconverged. At the end, Passmore thinks again of Egypt and its "indolent good-nature": "He thought of the silent, sun-baked quarries at Aswan . . . ; ruins sprouted in the desert of his mind—and desert it was. . . . He felt empty and naked. And nullity called to nullity. He yearned for the desert . . . [where] there was an escape from desire! . . . It was a barely concealed desire for sterility and even death and the realization was enough to make him search for at least one living being to share the solitudes with him" (302).

Paradoxically, that "one living being" is Guy, Passmore's dead double. The dead man, similarly to the dead woman in *The Young May Moon*, has loomed throughout the whole novel as a specter. Passmore's quest for life having now failed, the doubles Passmore and Guy, who are the quick and the dead, coalesce in an ironic form of reconciliation: "For it only required the ghostly presence of Guy to remind the living man there was nothing he wanted so much as to come into Guy's inheritance" (303). Passmore thereupon decides never to give up this quest, though he knows himself unneeded and unwanted by the Nashes. He has learned the truth, but he rejects it because his lethargic mind cannot accommodate change. The illuminating moment of self-knowledge is followed by an act of folly, self-deception. Passmore will continue his short time in England as a deliberately illusioned quester, reaching for life but drawing back at its touch. "Ah!" he perceived earlier at Whiteleaf, "to be unmolested the individual had to live alone, unloving and unloved" (204). So Egypt, with its enervating sun and sterile desert, will be his mirroring habitat. England could give him a season, but not a life.

As an exercise in the Jamesian mode, *A Season in England* is extremely interesting, particularly because the theme of the unlived life provided Newby a new approach to his by-now characteristic protagonist, the bewildered young man. But the novel contains problems, hardly Jamesian, that are not altogether successfully dealt with. First, the real center of interest—Passmore's realization and acknowledgment of his inability to *live*—is weakened by excessive development of material of subordinate interest and relevance. The background activity, as it were, distracts attention from the foreground; and the climax is obscured.

Many events twist and coil about, arousing expectation to little purpose beyond creating, redundantly, a sense of mystery. Early during his stay at Whiteleaf, Passmore (and, because of the Jamesian point of view, the reader too) is led to believe from remarks made by Mrs. Nash, who has not yet heard about Renee, that Guy had a wife and a child. Passmore is dumfounded and perplexed by what could be but is not an ironical *coup de théâtre*, and he works out various possible explanations, such as Guy's having been a bigamist or his first wife's having died. But Mrs. Nash's remarks, it turns out, were only reports of her overwrought imagination. This episode and others like it—especially that in which Mrs. Nash claims to have lost a wedding ring and causes everybody to look for it although she, unseen, has slipped it on one of her fingers—do not advance plot nor do they contribute anything necessary to characterization.

Finally, in a manner unworthy of Newby's Jamesian example, the novel is morally confused at its climax. Passmore is provided throughout with no convincing or acceptable moral foil (all the people are unsympathetic, insensitive, dotty, enigmatic, or amoral); and the reader is provided with no norm by which he can evaluate the man's character, apart from recognizing the negation of his embracing the desert world at the end. Renee ("reborn") is, to be sure, a contrast—the active female life-force. And certainly there is another contrast in the conspicuous example of masculine lust and lechery offered Passmore by that other mythic personage, that "devil with the women" Clegg (75), to whom he has been almost perversely attracted at Whiteleaf.

On the mythic level, then, Passmore fails in his quest for life when he does not, as Clegg would, make love to Renee in the hotel in London. But on the moral level the situation in the hotel has a different and contrary significance. In the first place, the situation is false since Renee has gone away with Passmore because she mistakenly believes that he tried to murder her. In the second and more important place, Passmore has desired marriage with Renee, not an affair; and an affair is all that the sensual Greek woman is willing to undertake. His behavior, the ironic reversal whereby he now rejects what he has strived to attain, condemns him on the mythic level; but it upholds and preserves his integrity on the moral level. The two levels do not merge, therefore, but collide at their coincidence; and the novel proceeds waveringly from this climactic impasse to an unsatisfactory, ambivalent conclusion. No question, in such a factitious circumstance, can be finally overwhelming.

CHAPTER 4

# School and War

W ITH *A Step to Silence* (1952) and its sequel, *The Retreat* (1953), Newby's career enters a new phase. These novels show a broadening of scope accomplished through the synthesis of former themes and techniques and the introduction of new ones. Having used the European war of 1939–1945 indirectly before, as in *Mariner Dances* and *The Snow Pasture*, Newby now deals direct- ly with that subject. In *A Step to Silence*, the war is an imminent threat that hovers on the borders of the characters' minds; in *The Retreat*, it becomes the major element of the plot. The prewar and wartime circumstances, as Walter Allen has observed, lift the action of these novels onto a wider plane and become almost characters themselves.[1] The private and public worlds are dynamically inter- related; more importantly for the theme, they are also reflecting parallels. The upheaval in the outer world corresponds, therefore, to the upheaval in the inner world, and to treat one is simultaneously to treat the other.

The subject of the public-personal relationship was evidently of urgent concern to Newby. Not only does he require two books to deal with it, but he treats it again, from different angles and with a different tone, in several later novels, most notably in *Something to Answer For* (1968). His preoccupation in *A Step to Silence*, in fact, is so studied that he employs obvious devices to highlight his points; and, as a consequence, this novel, despite many excellences, must rank as one of his least successful. Contrastingly, *The Retreat*, which is more imaginatively controlled and more objectively dis- tanced, is one of his masterpieces, flawed only in that its fullest effects cannot really be appreciated without reference to *A Step to Silence*.

Critics have not failed to mark this new phase in Newby's work. Although *A Step to Silence*, the first novel of the pair, was not published in the United States, *The Retreat* was and earned its author both more attention and more respectful praise than American critics had yet accorded him. To responsible commentators, such as Harvey Curtis Webster and Anthony West, *The Retreat* was a fulfillment of long promise.[2] And later English critics, such as Walter Allen and Anthony Burgess, devoted particular attention to these works of Newby's.[3]

## I  A Step to Silence

*A Step to Silence*, an initiation novel, is the story of a young man's unsettling journey from innocence to experience. During a period of less than a year, Oliver Knight moves from great expectations into a future that "seemed ordained and rational" (27), only to encounter upheaving disappointments, perplexity, loss of individuality, and isolation. The experience as a whole becomes for him but one long step to silence—the absence of answers to important questions raised along the way.

In the autumn of 1937, with portents of war abroad, Knight enters Mellingham, a teachers' training college—a choice determined financially by the recent death of his father. His attitude toward the school is condescending, but he participates wholeheartedly in the life there. He becomes the friend of a much older student, Martin Hesketh, who has led a varied life of odd jobs in many places in "the romantic world of experience" (177). Having decided to become a teacher, Hesketh has forced his admittance to the school, in spite of poor qualifications, by threatening to commit suicide if turned down. At Christmas, Knight joins his mother in Shropshire and first meets Jane Oliphant, a schoolteacher who has taken a room at Mrs. Knight's. Knight forms a warm, admiring attachment to this young woman. When Hesketh meets Jane, he too falls in love with her; and he eventually obtains her agreement to marry him. Meanwhile, he proves an unsuccessful student and, because of a suicide attempt and a brutal attack on another student, is dismissed from the college. Disillusioned more and more by the school, Knight rebels against its demands for conformity and decides that he too will leave at the end of the term. The narrative ends with Mrs. Knight's remarriage at Eastertime; and, despite his stepfather's offer to send him to Oxford University, Knight, "the person left out" (254), plans to join the air force.

Two elements dominate the novel, Mellingham and Hesketh. Walter Allen has commented about how the college functions as a metaphor of the state of the world and especially of the influence and workings of Fascism.[4] The school is self-inculpating: Newby convincingly depicts—through both events and images of severe disciplinarianism—how its insensitive, vulgar, and violence-dealing traditions, rules, rituals, and initiation ceremonies turn "individuals into members of a tribe" (43). Its academic standards are mediocre, and its required chapel attendance enforces a religion of bodies, not souls. The college patrols and discourages the students' relationships with the girls from the nearby sister training college; and it suspects its own students, like Knight and Hesketh, of homosexuality when they become friends. Knight "had always assumed that in some way knowledge was power and learning the pleasantest means of being different from the common run" (12–13). By demonstrating to him the callowness of this assumption, Mellingham provides Knight a first shocking encounter with ugly reality.

From Hesketh, Knight receives instruction in the variousness and contradictoriness of personality. An imperceptive student of this subject, Knight misunderstands even if he perceives the feelings, attitudes, ideas, and intentions of others. His failure is due partly to inexperience and partly to youthful self-centeredness. Cagily creating a paradox, Hesketh builds a friendship with the boy by making Knight responsible for him; and he superintends their relationship with loyalty and encouragement. (This segment of the plot climaxes in *The Retreat* when Hesketh finally carries out his threats of suicide and assumes responsibility for the death of Jane, thereby freeing Knight.)

Hesketh is one of Newby's finest creations; Walter Allen has called him "one of the best grotesques in contemporary fiction."[5] Complex, contradictory, inconsistent, exasperating, and wielding power through weakness, he is far more intricate than the Dickensian "humours" characters; but he is far less attractive than Newby's Mariner, from whom he is as surely descended as he is from Dickens's creations. Hesketh possesses as many negative as positive qualities; and, when Knight eventually but temporarily regards their relationship as merely an unsupportable burden, he is not guilty of immature lack of appreciation.

The very contrariness in Hesketh serves to influence Knight's inchoate human responses to other people. The two men are foils in many ways; and Hesketh, along with Jane, represents to Knight "the unknowability of the mature" (132). Hesketh has "dark intuitive knowledge" (132); and, with the force of that knowledge, he accurately accuses Knight of lacking feeling and of being cold and virginal. He is, says Hesketh, "an intelligence, not a man" (153).

An act of loyalty—impulsively defending Knight against some attacking fellow students—results in Hesketh's expulsion from Mellingham. Because he resents his friend's presumptuous interference, Knight emotionally rejects him. This response, also prolonged by jealousy of Jane, marks the turning point in Knight's rites of passage. Through Hesketh, he has discovered hate—human feeling—and he is now being prepared by this enlarging of response to meet future complications more equitably. He has learned something about himself (the real knowledge that is power) and about the world as well. It has an "ever-present possibility of violence" (184), and Knight knows that he is not immune to disaster.

Just as Hesketh's role is to develop Knight, so Jane's is to save Hesketh. She actively associates herself with religion; and, as "mistress of circumstances not their victim" (66), she is a figure of authority. In contrast with Knight, Hesketh understands people and circumstances intuitively; but Jane "knew what was happening because . . . she was a Christian" (132). And it is as a Christian that, even "if it damns her" (230), she is to save (in this novel) the soul of the unbeliever Hesketh. Moreover, being a "very strong character," as Hesketh's eccentric father calls her (230), Jane is just what the weak man needs—and deserves, too, according to his father—to be saved from himself for a workable existence in the everyday world. Although opposed to Jane's union with Hesketh, Knight nonetheless recognizes that his powerlessness to come between them is an "inescapable fact." This fact, importantly, "had expunged part of his childhood" (233).

*A Step to Silence* has, for a short novel, a large number of thematic concerns; but their presence is defensible because they represent the multifarious difficulties of growing up and living in the modern world. Knight, who says his situation is "the situation of us all" (206), must attempt to go forward step by step, in spite of impediments or restrictions of movement. The entire structure of the novel is subjected to an automatically frustrating irony that hampers movement, destroys the sense of direction, and empties traditional forms and significances of any positive meaning. For example, education does not teach, and its training is Fascistic (Mellingham "was not a place of learning, it was an institution" [13]).

Knight's educational experience is punctuated by Christmas and Easter; but, though acknowledging a vague religious feeling and a sense of mystery, he cannot accept the Christian faith, which he views as an "effective barrier to any true understanding of existence in this world": "The gulf between the Christian ideal and the observable facts was too great to be bridged" (81). The Christian holidays, therefore, merely grate against, instead of according with, his loss of belief in the future. Marriage, the sacrament of union, is for others, isolating Knight from them; and, from his mother's second marriage in the fruitful spring, "no child could be born" (250). Will is depicted as free, but its exercise is merely irrelevant or ineffectual in an age when, Knight asserts, "anything's possible" and "there aren't rules any more" (197). This opinion is refuted by Jane; but she herself, in this novel and particularly in *The Retreat*, is emphatically refuted by the unpredictability and swirling chaos of events. The handling of plot and characters thus becomes, by irony, an act of skeptical, sardonic contradictions.

In none of his novels has Newby so labored his thematic concerns as in *A Step to Silence*. Mellingham is weighted down with lustrous allegoric symbolism. Classrooms there are named after cities of antiquity—Athens, Ephesus, Babylon, Nineveh, Carthage, Rome; dormitories are named Valhalla and Paradise; a storage cellar, where the Jury, a secret student disciplinary committee, meets and passes sentences on offenders, is known as Hell. Likewise, much of the action, with its foreseeable futility, occurs in Worcester—the Faithful City. Toward the end of the novel, the omniscient narrator intrudes didactically: "Whatever the occasion for happiness let us not examine it too closely. Let us not hold it too firmly in our hands in case we crack the shell" (251). And a series of turgid passages, including a sermon, define, refine, and reiterate what can best be termed the message of the novel. Although some of this matter fits in dramatically, most of it nevertheless obtrudes artistically. The sermon serves to isolate and specify the theme of "innocence and experience" (210). Earlier in the novel, Newby has carefully defined innocence as a "state of not knowing," experience as a state of seeing "things as they were," and sentimentality as a "state of false knowing" (112). The following passage from the sermon develops theme in *fortissimo* tones:

It was the merest sentimentality to believe that ignorance of the ways of the world was, in itself, admirable. It was just as sentimental to imagine that we were contaminated by a knowledge of the ways of the world. Such beliefs postulated an unreal, untested, unimaginative innocence—indeed, an ignorance, which in present-day circumstances, as it happened, was all but impossible. Christianity was a practical faith, it dealt with things as they were. It was necessary to affirm, then, that the ever-widening circle of experience which was the lot of most of us came as a most powerful challenge. . . . "New ways, new people, new thoughts have to be met; if they mean anything to you at all they will reveal new worlds within yourself, and those worlds have to be conquered." (211)

In meeting this challenge, Knight ceases "to live in a divided world" (188–189). Personal experience is no longer private only; it is, rather, an aspect of a larger composite, as another passage shows:

There was no real division between private life and politics. Ignorance of one was ignorance of the other. The violence of a Hitler or a Mussolini could be understood by the violence of a Hesketh. This was not absurd. The newspapers and political commentaries could have no message for the unimaginatively innocent, and, short of the kind of awakening which only a war could bring, the personal crisis through which he passed was, for Knight, the only road to knowledge. If he was to be adult at this moment in history he saw how each and every act must, in some way, however remotely, be a political act; and . . . a religious one, too. (189)

A newspaper picture of Neville Chamberlain connects the public-private theme for Knight. This Prime Minister is an anachronism in the year 1938. To Knight, the head of the British government, like himself earlier, "appeared to take his own character and disposition as a piece of information about human affairs in general" (193). But Knight now knows better; he knows that "no one, not even those in the highest authority, was immune to innocence" (193). For such innocence is ignorance; and it causes one, disastrously, to try to live with illusion rather than to deal with reality, with things as they really are.

The end of the novel leaves Knight, despite this new knowledge, bewildered, as indeed it must if the historical allegory, or parallel, is to be valid, Reflecting on the sermon, he recalls that it said nothing "about what happened when you became another person" (212), which Christianity, in the terms of the novel as a "practical faith" that deals with things as they really are, should say. After all, Knight ponders, can't experience "rot the heart" (247)? He has two courses by which to find salvation: first, by "a deliberate act of the imagination" (228) to transform and thus transcend the hard facts of existence; second, to attempt "to understand the world and match that with right actions" (241). Although he might not have the right ideas, as Jane tells him, he is at least against the wrong ones. "It's enough to be going on with," she assures him; but, she adds, "it's only the beginning" (255).

## II   The Retreat

*The Retreat* is a story of flight and pursuit. The time is May, 1940. Knight has become a fighter pilot and has recently married. The novel opens with the undisciplined retreat of the British from France, and it is "every man for himself" (4). The ship carrying Knight across the Channel is bombed, and he is blown into the sea. All his documents and identity tabs are lost, and he gives the authorities a fictitious name, thus becoming "no one at all," a man "perfectly free" (36). Back in England, he does not go to Helen, his wife, but to Jane, who is now married to Hesketh, because he figures that, "if a meeting with Helen brought but the slightest intensification of his present feelings, he would crack" (42). He believes that Jane will be able to explain things to him and make sense of present confusion. But Jane herself needs help. Having given birth to a dead baby and being unable to have another child, she has become ill and disoriented; she is "as mad as you make 'em" and has "no sense of time or place" (99). When she and Knight go away together for a day, they decide not to return. Now follows a series of attempts by Hesketh, Helen, the civil and the military authorities to find the fugitive couple, who wander elusively from place to place. In the end, Jane dies (Knight later says that he murdered her); Hesketh commits suicide; and Knight rejoins Helen to find "sanctuary" (243) in her love.

In *A Step to Silence*, Knight recognizes the fact of violence in life; in *The Retreat*, he encounters and contends with it in the correlated private and public worlds. War is both external (men against men) and internal (man against himself). The retreat of the title of the novel is a collective reference to numerous increasingly complex retreats from violence, which are undertaken to remove or alleviate the pressures of time and circumstances. Life, as pointed out in *A Step to Silence*, is an indivisible composite of the public (social, political), the private, and the religious. Knight retreats from all three, and his retreats become the novel's organizing principle. The most obvious retreat is the actual military one from France. This event broadens to include Knight's retreat from the war altogether—general violence, not just one engagement. The fortuitous loss of official identification leads him into another retreat, the willful desertion of the air force, which he necessarily effects through the deliberate giving of a false name. Thus another retreat follows, that from the conscious, controlled self to the unconscious, impulsive self.

Public and private now overlap, and Knight retreats from his wife, who represents a personal relationship and personal obligation. He does not shun Helen because he does not love her but, in a paradoxical situation characteristic of all of Newby's fiction, because he *does* love her. He intends eventually to join her (he telegraphs her soon after reaching England); but he fervently feels that, psychologically and emotionally, he cannot do so immediately. He must prepare himself for their reunion, and he must take his time to do so. This retreat from Helen introduces two thematic strains, love and time, the importance of which emerges gradually.

Knight's meeting with Jane leads, ironically, to another, multifaceted retreat involving them both. Most simply, Jane uses Knight as a means of escape from Hesketh and from her life with him. For Knight, the situation is at first a reversal of intention; originally seeking comfort and advice from Jane, he is forced into assuming responsibility for her and her needs. This retreat becomes unpredictably but extremely treacherous because of the internal condition of both characters. Knight is in a state of shock as a result of the explosion on the ship (something, he says, "cracked in my mind" [72]); Jane is hopelessly demented. Creatures afflicted and maddened by public and private disasters, they function as figures symbolically embodying the chaos and anxieties of the age. What they desire is to retreat from reality and from time.

Fleeing reality, Jane attempts escape through death by trying to drown both herself and Knight when they are swimming in the sea. She has also attempted to escape by establishing a sexual relationship with Knight. Fleeing time, the couple seeks to retreat from the revolting present (which is reality) to the beautiful past (which is memory or illusion, both personal and mythological). "Oh God!" says Jane, "I wish we could put the clock back" (105). Newby develops this retreat by using, with ironic effect, the concept of prelapsarian man. Knight and Jane try to transfer themselves back to an Edenic state, a "state of grace" (206); they want to *reverse* the normal course of living and to journey backwards, away from experience, to innocence. (To do so, of course, is to escape both reality and responsibility according to terms set forth in *A Step to Silence.*)

This retreat is a culmination of the Edenic and pastoral motifs which run through both of these novels. In *A Step to Silence,* Jane and Knight have an important meeting in the Botanical Gardens, which is significantly a "favourite retreat" of Knight's (118). It is a Spenserian kind of microcosm since "every tree was different and labelled with its name and country of origin" (117). And, at the end of that novel, Knight relates a dream "in colour" that he once had about the coming of a timeless spring:

"First of all it was winter, . . . then . . . it was spring. It was just crinkling with green everywhere. The whole earth was green, north and south of the equator, all the seas, it was one big emerald. . . . The funny thing was that the earth stopped spinning when the spring began. . . . Oh, it was so beautiful and . . . when the earth stopped spinning and that rash of green spread everywhere, time itself had broken down. There was no more time. I felt as though I'd been let out of prison. The birds sang, the earth didn't revolve, the green light deepened—"

Here he says he woke up. And Jane comments, "So you see you can't escape from time" (252).

In *The Retreat,* Knight and Jane, ironic modern counterparts of Adam and Eve, are "lost in the wood" and "are trying to find [their] way." "We can scarcely see and we are afraid of feeling," says Knight. "And as we press on the trees are closing up behind us and barring our retreat. There is no retreat. We must go on and on" (111). In order to find their way, to reattain innocence and grace, they are even willing to offer a human life as a ritual sacrifice. Jane says that, when she ran away from Hesketh, she and Knight thought her husband would kill himself: "It seemed right for him to kill himself. I thought a sacrifice was wanted. A sacrifice would make everything clean again." Fittingly, Jane makes this statement in a garden "where an apple tree spread its branches," and she takes an apple, no bigger than a nutmeg, in her hand, "thinking of Eve and the Garden of Eden" (207).

Authoritative Jane in a visionary moment unites all these retreats by analyzing them in starkly religious terms: "I think . . . we're running away from God" (205). The point of this summary statement, which links personal, public, and religious together, is that separation, war, and guilt stem from the absence of personal and universal love. A person's rescue must necessarily be within the world of time since there is no retreat in that dimension ("you can't escape from time"), and it must be through love, which offers the seeker "sanctuary." Toward that, one "must go on and on."

A last retreat in the novel is Knight's retreat from Jane. The force that pulls him away from her and back to Helen is the force that rescues him: the force of love. This particular retreat has been prepared for by a series of repeated concrete symbols that indicate within themselves the conditions and mental states of both Knight and Jane. The first of these, significantly religious, is a group of nuns picnicking near a pond in an evacuated village which Knight passes through when retreating from France. There were two ducks on the pond, and Knight remembers this scene at the end of the novel when he sees two swans floating on a river: "The past and the present were knitting together, the wound was healing. Like the two ducks . . . , the swans became images of peace in a world at war. If he turned his head the nuns would drive up their car once more, and seating themselves on the green grass for a picnic, exorcise devils by the beauty of black gowns and starched white wings about pale faces" (267). This symbol, however, is not merely a facile evocation of peace; rather, it is insidious. Knight remains skeptical of the nuns, for they could have been German paratroopers in disguise. The ambivalence captures both Knight's wish for his wife and his fear of going directly to her.

The second symbol is a sea gull. Upon landing in England, Knight watches the flight of a gull until it disappears in the splendor of sunlight. Later, in mid-flight with Jane, he sees two gulls at the seashore. One of them is struggling to fly but cannot because its feathers have been gummed together with oil; the other one, nearby, is floating "sedately as a duck" (182). The crippled gull, obviously a parallel to Knight himself, also symbolizes, like the nuns, his wife. He responds to the gull with pity.

The third symbol presents a jolting configuration of Knight's situation. He finds a dead airman washed up on the rocks of the seashore near the gulls. The symbol reminds him immediately of his own figurative death when he was blown off the ship, and he attempts to recover the body (as he has attempted to rescue the oiled gull) in a gesture of self-recovery. "You're alive, Oliver," says Jane. "You're not in the sea. You don't have to go on looking for yourself in the sea like that" (228).

Last, a vixen acts as a symbol by which Knight is finally compelled and freed to retreat from Jane to Helen. The animal, which appears at a cottage where Knight and Jane have taken temporary shelter, symbolizes, immediately and obviously, the furtive, freedom-seeking couple themselves; but, as details about her cumulate, she takes on a more specific connotation. She is "on heat" but "out of season," and her wild screams indicate that she is "either mad or sick" (138). The connection between the vixen and Jane is obvious, for Jane in her final scene with Knight emits a cry that startles him "as the cry of the crazed vixen had startled him" (233).

The final scene between Knight and Jane is narrated in an oblique, truncated manner that necessitates its being interpreted simultaneously on the literal and symbolic levels. The actual setting and action, seen through the drunken and hysterical point of view of Knight, are transferred to the symbolic realm of the unconscious. It is night and a storm is approaching, and Knight and Jane are in a dark hotel room by the sea (there are no lights because of the blackout). Jane, described metaphorically as a threatening creature of evil, is the temptress who is keeping the hero from returning to his beloved wife; the "witch," in Helen's terms, whose "enchantment" of Knight "had to be broken" (101). Night is "her natural element" (232), and she goes out into the whirling winds and water of the storm to watch the lightning. When Knight assaults her in sexual passion, she for the first time resists him and tells him to return to Helen. He retorts by exclaiming, in a symbolic reference to the predatory, sick vixen, "You bitch! Let me go!" And Jane dissolves in his grip "like a wraith" (234). Hesketh then enters the room and, after going over to his supine, mute wife, he sends Knight away: "Go away quickly now. . . . You must get out of the hotel without being heard. I want them to find just the two of us together" (235).

Knight departs, knowing that Jane is dead; and, though the police decide that the self-slain Hesketh murdered her, Knight declares later that he killed her. The omniscient narrator never makes an unequivocal statement that clears up the matter, and the language used for reporting events themselves, as well as other passages dealing with the subject, is so surrealistic and elliptical that it defies certainty. This uncertainty was probably Newby's precise and ingenious intention. At any rate, this particular treatment of language is not a pointless clever trick but a means of placing the reader in the same predicament as the characters.

The fact of Jane's dying is what is important. Whether Knight actually killed her or not, he does kill her subconsciously. Before being able to go to Helen, he must free himself of the power of Jane established in *A Step to Silence* and exercised so obsessively in *The Retreat*. The association in his subconscious mind of the premonitory symbol of the vixen with Jane ("You bitch!")—thus merging the two narrative levels as well as the two levels of mind—allows him at last to break loose and frees him finally to act independently, to make his last retreat.

Now liberated both from and by the Heskeths, Knight can review his experience and seek meaning in it. In recapitulating the series of retreats, he pulls together themes, motifs, and symbols of both *A Step to Silence* and *The Retreat:* "In that moment the happenings of the past few days appeared to Knight a mysterious ritual. The flight itself, the scream of the vixen in the moonlight, the distressed gull, the dead airman, the ordeal in which Jane and he had nearly drowned, his own dream [about time], and Jane's confronting the storm . . . —all these seemed the movements of a ceremony for the composure of troubled spirits. And it had ended here and now in this moment of silence" (237–238).

These two novels make an interesting unit. The first, concerned with the future, relentlessly propels Knight forward—is a step *to;* the second, concerned with the past, drives him back—is a retreat. He has thus not progressed at all; and he is as bewildered at the conclusion as at the beginning. He remains unable to locate in the world, whether divided or not, certainty, order, or rationality.

Religion, like other systems, offers in these novels no assistance in a world that has lost faith. Its worthiest believer, Jane, abandons her faith, which was the source of her "true ascendancy" (109) over Knight, and she tumbles into desperation because Christianity has not proved for her a practical religion. The church "meant nothing to her any more" (197); and God, she says, has not helped her in her need as she had thought since childhood that He would. Unable to face things as they really are, unable to be faithful to Christianity, which in *A Step to Silence* she saw as "sternly realistic" (81), she falls victim to madness, sexual obsession, and finally death.

Jane changes from spiritual independence to sexual dependence in a vertical narrative movement that contrasts with the forward-backward movement of Knight's jerky bewilderments. Moreover, her decline, by being depicted within a Christian framework, has a bitterly tragic ironic significance. In *A Step to Silence*, this spiritual woman, with whom, just after meeting her, Knight goes to a church at Christmas to set up a Nativity scene, contrasts cruelly with the later woman who bears a dead baby and can never conceive again. In *The Retreat*, Jane's reference to herself—a deranged, barren woman—in terms of Eve, the first mother, is made as part of a "confession" (205) in a counterfeit, dusky garden to a contemptible landlady who upbraids her for adultery with Knight. Setting and circumstance mock Jane's experience and her "confession," and the resultant irony enforces a painful sense of loss.

Despite the ineffectiveness of religion, love—the foundation and the teaching of the Christian faith—remains the only "sanctuary." And this sanctuary offers Knight a kind of salvation which he can find: "Can't we just be with each other?" he asks Helen. Then:

His heart moved. When the first violent throb had died away he put a hand out to Helen. He faced her. The blue eyes, he saw, were as wild as his own.

Momentarily her strength failed; she looked away. But his cry of pain brought the eyes back again. He found himself silently calling on God to give him strength enough to meet those eyes; he called noiselessly on angels for support. Then, as suddenly as it had begun, the ordeal was over. For the second time Jane made her strange remark, that they were running away from God; Hesketh himself parted the curtain of fire, and Knight finding himself on the other side, saw the face of a woman who was in all blessed certainty his wife. They clung to each other, shivering.

"Did you know what I meant by sanctuary?" he asked.

At last she said, "I think so." (271)

Paradoxically, this is retreat at the end of retreat.

The conclusion of these two novels is disconsolate and darkly depressing. Like Matthew Arnold's "Dover Beach," it expounds the necessity of mutual faith in personal relationships in a world far removed from its golden age and lacking certitude, peace, and help for pain: "Ah, love, let us be true / To one another!" But Newby disturbs even the chilly serenity of this resting point. Knight the innocent boy has become Knight the experienced fighter in a world of confused alarms of struggle and flight, of ignorant armies clashing by night. Motion is perpetual; there is no final cadence. There is no retreat.

## CHAPTER 5

# Egypt and Britain

*T*HE *Picnic at Sakkara* (1955), *Revolution and Roses* (1957), and *A Guest and His Going* (1959) constitute a trilogy, and they have a twofold importance in Newby's career.[1] They are his first works of laughing comedy. They are also his first direct and extensive treatment in fiction of the Egyptian character which had made such a "determinate impression" on him during his stay in the Middle East during the early 1940's.[2] An essay on the Oriental character which Newby published in 1949 provides a helpful introduction to these novels.[3] Whether Egyptian, Greek, Armenian, Jew, or Syrian, the most particularly fascinating trait of the Oriental, says Newby, is his shamelessness—his candid acceptance of all men as "human beings with human appetites and human weaknesses." These people assume that human beings have much more in common than not, and they recognize therefore no mysteries nor hidden motives in human behavior. In *The Picnic at Sakkara*, one character says that "in Egypt there are no secrets. Everyone is outspoken" (183). In this way the Oriental contrasts with the Englishman, who is interested in individuality and eccentricity. With no need of being reserved, the Oriental can give full play to his curiosity about others; contrastingly, the Englishman, determined to guard his own unique personality, has difficulty in getting to know others and in establishing personal relationships.

Newby turned his attention in this trilogy to this subject of Orientals and Englishmen, and he built each of the three novels upon the conflict that results when these two strikingly different types, the Eastern and the Western, meet. In these novels, he continues to use the theme of public and private relationships which so engaged him in the two Oliver Knight novels, but he now views that theme in terms much more specifically political. Again the juxtaposed fictional and historical patterns are self-reflecting. As he observes in *A Guest and His Going*, "In a time of gloom and crisis quite small happenings take on the import of symbols" (158).

The trilogy is, therefore, unified thematically; and it actually provides a fictional review in the comic mode of a decade of Anglo-Egyptian relationships. *The Picnic at Sakkara* is set in Cairo in 1946, during the reign of King Farouk, when the nationalists are calling for the unity of the Nile Valley and the withdrawal of British forces. *Revolution and Roses* is set in Alexandria in 1952 during the week of the revolution under General Naguib that forced King Farouk's abdication. *A Guest and His Going* is set in London in 1956 during the crisis following President Nasser's nationalization of the Suez Canal. The real protagonists of these novels may well be said to be Britain and Egypt, and the primary interest shifts rather markedly from the personal-fictional level in the first novel to the political-historical level in the third.

## I   *A Comic World*

The narrative movement of each of these novels is comedic, going from intricate complication to simplified resolution with the main characters attaining or reattaining the balanced existence and outlook of the happy ending. Husband and wife are reconciled in *The Picnic at Sakkara;* lovers are united in *Revolution and Roses;* and an outsider is reclaimed by society in *A Guest and His Going*.

The characters, all of them, are static; they do not grow or undergo a change. They collide with one another.[4] They are embroiled in events from which they must extricate themselves by the exercise of ingenious wit or, more often, from which they are extricated by some agent of good fortune. The pleasure and ultimately the meaning of these three novels derive, therefore, from the external, not the internal, action. With skillful mastery, Newby has created a comic world populated by a large number of distinctive character-types who are involved in a copious variety of ridiculous situations and farcical incidents.

Everything is controlled by a benevolent comic irony that is critical only to the extent that all irony implies criticism. Events and situations derive their humor from incongruities and from often unpredictable outcomes. Life in this comic world is absurd, as a character observes in *A Guest and His Going;* anything can happen, and anything is possible, as another character recognizes in *The Picnic at Sakkara*. "Anything can happen" in the Oliver Knight novels also, but the inconsequence of events is bitter and tragic; in the trilogy what happens is jocose and comic. The characters amuse through arousing anticipation (we know how, being types, they will clash) and through surprise (being inconsistent, especially the Orientals, they often reverse expectation). Only in *A Guest and His Going*, with one man's anfractuous passage into madness, does the humor swerve toward the tragic. The major characters of the trilogy are fully indentured to the service of theme, but the minor characters, like a kind of comic chorus, engage in activities that emphasize for hilarious purposes the incongruities inherent in, and caused by, men's perennial follies, vanities, and frailties.

## II   The Picnic at Sakkara

The central characters of *The Picnic at Sakkara*[5] are Edgar Perry, an Englishman who teaches at Cairo University; his wife Mary; and Muawiya Khaslat, one of Perry's Egyptian students. As a result of investigating students' living conditions, which he wants to see improved, Perry becomes involved in a riot and is arrested. When Muawiya secures his release from custody, he thus becomes Perry's rescuer for a second time. Earlier Muawiya had saved Perry from the violent dangers of a student demonstration, thereby creating a bond between himself and his teacher. In order to express appreciation to Perry for his concern about the welfare of the students, a group of them invite him and Mary to go on a picnic at Sakkara. There among the ancient tombs, acting on orders from the nationalistic Moslem Brotherhood of which he is a member, Muawiya attempts to assassinate Perry. Failing, he proclaims that he has saved Perry from committing suicide. Because of the possibility of his becoming a controversial political figure, the university dismisses Perry; and he and Mary plan to return to England. On the train taking them away, Muawiya joins them with a basket of food; and all three of them eat "from the outskirts of Cairo to Benha and beyond" (239).

The theme of public and private, national and personal loyalties emerges effortlessly from the development of this plot. The personal experiences of Perry, an affable and well-intentioned but mild, irresolute, and misguided man, parallel the confusion in the public sphere. His myopia is symbolic as well as literal; and, although he "liked to boast he was as blind as a bat without his glasses," he is "short-sighted" (26) even when he has them on and stumbles from one farcical situation into another. He himself recognizes that "like a hero of classical antiquity he lived in a world of histrionic irony where other people knew more about his situation than he knew himself" (170).

His relationship with Mary is uncertain, and he cannot decide how best to deal with her. She has joined him after a separation of several years caused by the war, but she is fearful that Perry does not love her as much as she loves him (he is eight years older than she). Upon her arrival in Cairo, she tells him that she has a lover in England to whom she is engaged and that she wants a divorce; Perry does not know that this is a "monstrous lie" (50). Yet Mary finds that her husband has attractively changed during their separation; he is now "more direct, more frank in his manner" (47); and she allows him to make love to her. The traditional comedic theme of marital infidelity is clearly due for a surprising twist here, and connubial bliss is reestablished only after a series of misunderstandings and illusions that lead the English couple about in a ludicrously comic circle.

The ambiguity of the Perrys' relationship is finally resolved when Mary misinterprets Muawiya's false report of what happens at Sakkara. She believes that Perry is in despair over her intention to divorce him and that he has resorted to suicide because of his love for her. Now convinced of his devotion, she openly declares her real feeling for him, calling him "darling" for the first time since their reunion. Perry has, of course, remained in love with his wife and resents her misinterpretation of the events at the picnic, but he is nonetheless willing not to disillusion her: "If he was not a repentant suicide what was he? The difficulty of thinking up some other role defeated him" (166).

This personal bewilderment also exists in Perry's public life as a professor in a city where "political demonstrations of one sort or another were a daily occurrence" (19) and where students are as likely to attack as to flatter or befriend. A nonpolitical act, like Perry's attempt to obtain better dwellings for students, can instantly become a political one in support of any faction according to the coign of vantage from which that act is viewed. In private life, Perry is not clear whether he is to remain a husband or is about to become a divorcé; in public life, whether he is a friend or an enemy.

The public situation is the thematic heart of the novel, just as the picnic is the central event. At the same time that the students are giving the picnic as a gesture of appreciation and homage to Perry as a champion of their rights, Muawiya is preparing to act against Perry, his friend. The reason for the attack is political: the Moslem Brotherhood has ordered the murder as a test of Muawiya's loyalty. Perry has always failed to understand Muawiya's position as a patriot, despite warnings of his potential danger. "Sir," says Muawiya to Perry, "you must have no wrong ideas about me. I am a patriot. You must not trust me" (72). Actually, Muawiya does not shoot; but, while Perry is wresting the pistol away from him, it goes off and scorches the side of Perry's face. To save himself with honor from this fiasco, Muawiya reports to the picnickers that he has stopped Perry from doing away with himself, and another false situation develops. For Perry to tell the truth about what happened would bring to Muawiya not only disgrace but hardship, probably a long prison term; therefore, goodhearted Perry remains quiet.

But, since "anything can happen," another ridiculous situation develops. Muawiya is jailed after all; and Perry, trying to secure his release, speaks up for him. The assassination failed only because of bad luck, Perry tells the police; and he testifies that, as a matter of fact, Muawiya is "a damn good assassin and I don't bear him any ill will" (223).

The comic irony has not yet run its sinuous course. When Muawiya breaks out of jail, he goes to Perry for a climactic confrontation and charges Perry with having mocked him to his friends by terming him a good assassin. To set matters straight, he demands of Perry, "Confess you are my enemy" (231). Muawiya is finally placated when Perry says that he and Mary are returning to England. "Let God be praised! We have driven the English to the sea!" (233), exclaims Muawiya. In this scene Perry's thoughts are instrumental in stabilizing the theme of private-public conflict on the level of politics: "Why should Muawiya want hatred from him? Did friendship with an Englishman make life impossibly difficult? Did it cloud his allegiances? Did it confuse motives? Did it make too difficult the path of the patriot?" (231).

In the anterior scene of the "grave crisis" at Sakkara, Perry has already reflected on this "perfect illustration of the twentieth-century dilemma." According to his view, "Man was a political animal. He was also a human being. When, in one individual, these two characters come into conflict—as happened at Sakkara—the outcome was inevitably muddled" (157). Muawiya is, therefore, a notable example of the modern divided man whose loyalties on the public and the private plane conflict.

To the Brotherhood, however, Muawiya is quite simply not a good patriot. "To be a good patriot," says one of their members to Perry, "one must be realistic. [Muawiya] is not realistic. He is sentimental. . . . He failed [in his mission to kill you]. He does not understand the twentieth century" (215). This man, a spokesman of modern nationalism as opposed to nineteenth-century imperialism, asks for undivided loyalties in an age of violence: "It is not that we do not like you. We kill you because we are opposed to your country's policy. Personal feelings do not come into the matter. Some Egyptians believe that they can like individual Englishmen and hate England. Now we, in the Brotherhood, do not believe that" (213).

Ironically, Perry is capable of only an unequivocal response to this dilemma. He tells Mary that "ever since I arrived in this country I've been walking the back of a knife. Extraordinarily hard to keep a balance. I can't be neutral. I can't be passive. Either I hate the country or I like it very much. Either I loathe my students or I admire them. If I don't feed my admiration and—yes, love if you like—I could easily fill up with hate" (45). In this comic world of contradictions, the student Muawiya by the exercise of his Oriental imagination survives the test of loyalty by seeing Perry as not continuously a friend-enemy but as now a friend, now an enemy—by seeing the separate parts, not the whole. As F. X. Mathews has explained, "Whatever [Muawiya] feels or imagines at the moment is reality; consistency is irrelevant to truth."[6] Thus he can both loathe and love: "Sir, I love you as a man but I hate England" (68).

No small part of the piquant humor of this novel derives from episodes that recount Perry's farcical relationships with Egyptians other than Muawiya. Perry has as little success in making sense and order at the university as he does at home, but one of many examples illustrates this situation. When one of his classes is interrupted by an inrushing group of students who are making political protests, Perry orders the agitators from the room and calls them hooligans—"only to see the word taken down in a notebook by one of the Saudi Arabians" (21). In the tumultuous confusion that develops, one of these students says in Perry's ear, "Sir! . . . What is the etymology of this word 'hooligan'?" (22).

Likewise, the subplot involving the aged Princess—the "Conscience of Egypt"—and her husband Tureiya Pasha con- tributes a cardinal pleasure to the comic world of bafflement in which Perry and Mary are caught. This regal Oriental husband and wife, who exist in a gaudy world of dreams and illusions of power, are attended in the hubbub of their establishment by an English butler who has a "Tyneside accent even after thirty years in Egypt" (12). ("Mary knew she was in the presence of royalty because there was no sense of privacy" [75].) The Pasha has hired Perry to give him private English lessons, but "His Excellency took up all the time chattering in French, saying that he wanted a friend, not an English teacher" (9). The feminist Princess, who has had three husbands, becomes Mary's confidante and applauds her for break- ing Perry's spirit. To Mary's reply, "Oh no. Don't say that. He loves me," comes the majestic riposte, "It is the same thing" (174).

Newby uses the stylized high jinks of the Princess and the Pasha to indicate, with a bland irony, the basic frivolity and uselessness of their vain and luxurious life. But he never allows such humorous commotion to obscure his theme or to distort the structure of the novel. The structure, as is typical of his carefully molded narratives, does not merely contain the theme; its form is its meaning.

The picnic at Sakkara is duplicated by the picnic on the train, and the differences are as telling as the similarities. At Sakkara, the relationship between Perry and Muawiya reaches a point of necessary definition. Unlike the event at the picnic in *A Passage to India*, which it inevitably brings to mind, this event is not shrouded in a never-resolved mystery. What happens at Sakkara is perfectly clear to the reader: Muawiya deliberately mismanages the assassi- nation; he gives Perry not only a warning but time and opportunity to react as well. The jarring double role of patriot and friend momentarily immobilizes Muawiya; though the patriot prepares to act, the friend checks the action; consequently, "the outcome was inevitably muddled" (157). But the situation clarifies that the relationship between the Englishman and the Egyptian cannot be cemented into an adhering block; they cannot in reality conjoin on the private and public planes simultaneously; but they can be departmentalized and balanced within the imagination of affection. Thus on the train, in light of this violently forced truth, Muawiya can freeheartedly entertain the Perrys because they are now departing guests, not interfering colonials. They can come together at the end as personal friends, though paradoxically they must remain public enemies. In a way, this situation is a dramatic realization of the Pasha's reference to perpetual motion on the first page of the novel; hence, its occurrence is not a mere formal duplication of the picnic at Sakkara. The second picnic perforce calls up the first, and the juxtaposition both narratively and thematically defines the whole dilemma dramatized in the novel and the balance toward which it moves. It is a triumph of the imagination, both Newby's and the characters'. Perry decides: "Perhaps [Muawiya] really was the force that drove [me] all the way back to England. But it was not intimidation. It was deep regard, shot through with jealousy; an abortive love affair" (234). And Muawiya, "so carried away" that he can "scarcely tell dream from reality," says: "We [Egyptians] talk wonderful things and we understand them. We have more sense of humour and more imagination than other people. Every day we say the English are gone! One day, who knows, they will be!" (234–235).

### III   Revolution and Roses

The only character from *The Picnic at Sakkara* in the second novel of the trilogy, *Revolution and Roses,* is Waldo Grimbley, formerly head of Perry's department at the university in Cairo. The Egyptian nationalists have turned him out of his job, along with all other British officials in government pay; and Grimbley is now temporarily employed as Acting Vice-Consul at the British Embassy in Alexandria. The action centers, however, on the activities of Elaine Brent and Lieutenant Mahmoud Yehia. Elaine, a journalist on holiday, lands without a permit in Alexandria to "scoop" the events of the revolution which has just begun. She leaves ship with Tim Blainey, who has come to Egypt to visit his half-brother Eric and to gather experience so that he can become a writer "sceptical and worldly-wise like Mr. Somerset Maugham" (83).

Eric is married to Lydia, the daughter of Paulos Dragoumis, a

Greek merchant and amateur philosopher with whom Eric is in business. When Yehia catches the landing party going ashore, he falls immediately and hopelessly in love with Elaine. During the night, when Farouk escapes from confinement in Montazah Palace, Yehia is courting Elaine; and, though officially off duty, he considers himself disgraced because he has neglected his patriotic duty for a woman. Elaine is taken to be the foreign lady who is rumored to have helped Farouk escape by seducing an Egyptian soldier; she is detained but is eventually released. Yehia hopes to redeem his honor by taking a royalist stronghold without bloodshed, but his overzealous actions cause several men, including himself, to be wounded. Elaine sails away on the yacht carrying Farouk into exile. Later Yehia goes as a military attaché to London and there recommences his courtship of Elaine.

The public-private conflict is the unifying theme also of *Revolution and Roses*, and it is exemplified in the doings and misdoings of Yehia, "a lover and a republican" (201). The title of the novel unites in itself the two conflicting forces: the revolution in which Yehia as a loyal Egyptian nationalist is taking part and the roses which he sends to Elaine in his courtship of her. In short, Yehia is caught between war and love in the service of two mistresses, Egypt and Elaine. "This woman," he says, "is almost as important to me as my country. . . . I am at the crisis of my life. Revolution and this woman!" (66). Yehia asks Elaine's young friend Tim how to court her, and Tim advises him to send flowers. So Yehia sends roses to Elaine, dozens of them, while in his mind the soldiers of his platoon detailed for General Naguib's guard of honor are "Egyptian flowers" that are collectively Yehia's "posy at the feet of the General" (99).

This novel contrasts with *The Picnic at Sakkara* in that it is quite self-consciously literary. The diverting and amusing complexities of surface action constitute a burlesque of medieval romance, and this old tradition illuminates a perhaps otherwise obscured dimension of the composition of the novel. This humorous mismatching of medieval and modern, like the perilous union of Egyptian and Englishman, makes of disorder a thoroughgoing organizing principle. As a result, Yehia is more than a professional soldier, and Elaine is more than a professional woman. He is the idealistic knight errant; she, his lady. He is fully committed to the occupations of performing deeds of valor and of wooing, and he is bound in both the private and the public areas of his life by the code of loyalty.

The comedy results from several ironic variations on the old romance tradition. First, Newby transfers this European literary practice to the East, thereby confusing the lover in his attempts to win the lady by a method foreign to him. In his quest, he is driven to seek aid and advice about "how to please this woman" (66) according to the rituals of European courtship from the innocent, inexperienced Tim, who, ironically, fancies himself to be a candidate for Elaine's amorous favors. This already incongruous situation is futher complicated by the polar national differences between Yehia the Oriental and Elaine the Occidental. Yehia's dilemma is rendered especially ironic by the fact that, "*wildly* in love" (129), he is a citizen of a Moslem country where "they don't take women seriously. They're too realistic" (74).

Yet Yehia is wholeheartedly smitten by Elaine and her blue eyes: "For Yehia she had represented a new sense, as distinct as hearing or vision; at her touch the whole world had been shaken, opening treasure grottoes in the rock" (101–102). And, in answering the question where he first met her, he attaches the importance of a goddess to her. " 'In the sea,' said Yehia. 'She came up from under the water. I saw the sun shining into her face, like brightness in a cloud' " (102).

Politically, Yehia finds his romancing almost impossible. According to the chivalric code, love of woman inspires in her suitor devotion to his king; but, in this farcical romance of the rose, Yehia as a militant revolutionist is working with a group trying not only to rid Egypt of its king but also to liberate the country from British oppression. Attentions to Elaine remove Yehia from the scene when the king escapes—"I am a soldier of Egypt and I have failed my country in the hour of destiny! And for a woman!" he wails (100)—and then force him into the role of protector when she is falsely arrested. Although "there was little enough nobility in the world, and heroes were out of fashion" (150), Yehia nonetheless behaves with nobility.

Another of the ironically comical reversals of the romance tradition is the age of the lovers, for neither of them is still young. Elaine will be thirty-two on her next birthday, "getting on for middle-age and still unmarried" (228); and Yehia is thirty-three. Physically, however, they are stereotypical. Elaine is "as fresh as a dairymaid, with pale, swimming eyes and a scatter of freckles at the temples" (9). Yehia is "tall, handsome," with red skin, a face of "unusual width at the cheekbones, making an impression of great strength" (31), and a fine chest covered with "coppery . . . hair, very thick and shiny" (149).

Ironically, Elaine ill fits the role of romance heroine in two other ways. First, she is sexually self-conscious:

> Men, she thought, men—why are they afraid of me back home? Not so much me, perhaps, but any woman of thirty. Why do the unmarried ones look on any gesture of friendliness as an attempt to seduce them into marriage? She had seen, as a result of her smile, real panic in a bachelor's eyes. Perhaps he had cause. The reason why Englishmen as a whole had such fear of spinsters, she decided, lay in their respectability. Their thoughts turned with heavy inevitability to marriage. . . . Elaine, her mind working on men . . . , considered with some joy her entry into a society where men were not sexually respectable but unafraid and courteous. (93)

Yehia, one gathers, has led a celibate's life, having dedicated himself "to the service and to the liberation of Egypt" (66). But Mrs. Dragoumis represents the stock response to Egyptian lovers. "Yellow roses from an Egyptian!" she exclaims in horror as she explains to her daughter. "When you are as old as I am, . . . you will know what it means, yellow roses from an Egyptian, and you will be sick in your stomach as I am now" (122).

Mrs. Dragoumis is instrumental, in her finest hour, in bringing to the fore the second reason Elaine is but an ironical heroine of romance. Traditionally, just as the lady inspires the knight to devotion to king and country, so does she inspire him to devotion to God; but Elaine is not a Christian. When she and Mrs. Dragoumis are caught between the opposite forces of the revolution one night and are likely to be killed, the Greek woman tries to persuade Elaine to make a last-minute conversion and become a martyr:

> As Mrs. Dragoumis fought for Christ she was happy as she had never been happy before. It was self-evident. This was her moment of fulfilment. Marriage, childbirth were as achievements insignificant in comparison. She stepped out of the boredom of Alexandria into triumph. "So little is asked,"

she said [to Elaine], "and the reward is so great."
"No, I'm not a Christian," said Elaine, turning mulish. (187)

The outcome is not death and martyrdom for Christ but rescue by a "magnificent [Egyptian] officer, seemingly eight feet tall" (188). Ever after, Mrs. Dragoumis, left a psychosomatic invalid by the anticlimax, says dismissively of Elaine, "A pretty young woman, but an atheist" (240).

Finally, Yehia "the man and the patriot could act in harmony" (201). For to take Ras el-Tin Palace, where both Farouk and Elaine are believed to be, would at one blow destroy the king and release Elaine, thereby restoring Yehia to public and private honor after his recreance the night Farouk escaped. It is characteristic of the shaping irony of surprise and inconsequence in this trilogy and of the mode of burlesque in this particular novel that the attack turns out quite differently from what is expected: the chivalric expectations are thus yet again turned upside down. The knightly daring deed fails through excess of valor; and the foolhardy soldier, upon seeing the venerated lady, gives her not a kiss but a spit in the face. Before their reconciliation in England at a later time, Yehia writes to Elaine, as to a kind of *belle dame sans merci*, asking her permission for him to come to London. When he at last arrives there, he rejoins her to the accompaniment of music being played in a Nonconformist chapel next door to her flat. The quest, burlesqued in terms of medieval romance, thus carries through to its traditional ending.

The structure of *Revolution and Roses* is much looser than that of *The Picnic at Sakkara* in spite of this narrative quest-pattern. The reader's movement through its episodes and his meeting its characters are rather like a progress through a disordered funhouse. One of the most amusing attractions is old Mr. Dragoumis. He asks, "Why is Alexandria known to the world?" and answers, "Because of its philosophers" (129). He writes letters in Greek to famous people throughout the world for help with his "entirely novel philosophy of politics" (21) at which he has labored for many years:

And when the replies came (as very occasionally they did) Mr. Dragoumis ascribed their brevity and general unsatisfactoriness to the decline of Greek as a learned tongue and the unprecedented nature of the problems he was tackling. Even H. G. Wells was baffled. Shortly before his death he wrote to Mr. Dragoumis saying: "I have had your letter translated and all I can say is that you are well-intentioned." Mr. Dragoumis was delighted with the compliment. But, to be frank, Wells had not been a help. Repeated disappointments of this kind would naturally postpone the completion of his work. (22)

As to Mrs. Dragoumis, the Christian crusader, she is "jealous of the attention her husband gave to the affairs of mankind" (23).

The revolution itself is farcical. "A war in which there were two sides only," the narrator reports, "was too much to hope for: being Egyptian, the affair would necessarily be complicated" (157). And a confused Egyptian official says, "In this country today we do not know who our masters are. Perhaps the English will occupy Cairo once more" (54). Such was not, of course, to happen. In reviewing this novel Norman Podhoretz commented perceptively that "it is the Egyptians who have had the last laugh; their 'silly' revolution has had momentous consequences for the world, and particularly for the British." He observes that Newby, "an Englishman whose business is humor," could not have been insensitive to this irony, but that "it is not obtrusive in his book."[7] Nor should it be, since Newby's aim has been "to show ordinary human relationships" by use of "the traditional material of love and 'a-political' adventure." The revolution, whatever the magnitude of its consequences, is just another of the lenses through which Newby views the ever enigmatical relationships of people in this comic world where anything is possible.

## IV    A Guest and His Going

In *A Guest and His Going*, Newby assembles in London most of the characters from the two preceding novels; only Eric, Lydia, and Mr. and Mrs. Dragoumis are missing. Perry is now head of a language school for foreign students which is housed in Napier Hillingdon's residence, Helvetia, in Hampstead Garden Suburb; and Grimbley, who has "suffered a real comedown in the world" (23), is his senior assistant. Muawiya has arrived in England for a visit as a guest of the British Council, for which Tim now works.

In the course of a party given for him by Mrs. Blainey, Tim's mother, Muawiya (unlicensed to drive) goes off in Hillingdon's car (uninsured), wrecks it, and escapes the police by taking refuge in the Egyptian Embassy—which denies his being there. If the British authorities caught him, Muawiya says, they would persecute him unjustly because of the anti-Egyptian attitudes aroused by the Suez crisis. He nonetheless manages to host and attend a party that Perry arranges for him; to engage in a debate on the subject of the brotherhood of men, held by a private society; and to address the crowds at Speakers' Corner in Hyde Park.

There, Muawiya, having himself notified the police and the press of his planned appearance, is finally arrested. Perry pays his bail and allows him to stay at Helvetia until his hearing. The charges against Muawiya are dismissed, but he is enraged that he has not been imprisoned because his entire effort to become a political martyr, which has all along been his plan, has failed. Nobody, he says, can "have a political career nowadays without being a martyr first of all" (144). He returns to Egypt, declaring that he likes England, that he has enjoyed his visit, and that he would like to return someday as ambassador.

In *A Guest and His Going*, the political situation of confusion, distrust, and apprehension created by Nasser's seizure of the Suez Canal is reflected in the personal situations. "That was the trouble with English people these days," one reads. "They could never disentangle political from personal relationships" (4). This situation is developed with humorous irony that plays up the contrast and the discrepancy in understanding between the "shameless" Orientals and the secretive English characters. A wide sea of misunderstanding flows between the principal representatives of each nationality, and communication itself is seldom established.[8]

Grimbley, Hillingdon, and Mrs. Blainey all contribute importantly to this situation. In *The Picnic at Sakkara*, Grimbley tries "to lead the life of a well-to-do Egyptian of a hundred years ago" (38); and, in *Revolution and Roses*, "filled with delight . . . at the confusion of the country that had injured him," he excitedly sees Elaine's being a prisoner of the Egyptians as "an admirable pretext for taking this bloody country over again" (158, 162). But, by the time of his arrival at Helvetia in *A Guest and His Going*, he has come to hate the Egyptians so much that he insists none ever be enrolled as students in the school. "Grimbley hated the Egyptians," Perry thinks, "because he really loved them; indeed, wanted to *be* an Egyptian" (22).

94

P. H. NEWBY

Corpulent Hillingdon goes to the dowager Mrs. Blainey to seek her advice; yet, before he can begin, she urges him to drop charges against Muawiya for wrecking his car in order to protect the career of her son Tim, who, through his position with the British Council, had been responsible for Muawiya. Mrs. Blainey is constantly using Hillingdon's courtship of her as a means of exploiting him; the situation exposes the general misunderstandings in relationships prevalent in this fictional comic world:

Only the day of the party Elaine had accused [Mrs. Blainey] of exploiting poor Napier. He was forever shopping, cutting dead wood out of the wistaria, polishing silver, moving furniture; but, as Mrs. Blainey pointed out, it was embarrassing to have such a big man standing about and saying nothing; she suggested these little jobs as a form of amusement for him. And, of course, it certainly made his presence more attractive to her. Apart from his usefulness it was as though the atmospheric pressure was reduced when he was found a job to do. If it weren't for the jobs he would give her the most terrible, oppressive headache. Exploitation was a silly way to describe all the consideration Napier received in her house. (139)

Once, when he goes to warn Mrs. Blainey that Muawiya is dangerous, Hillingdon finds the man in hiding at her house; to alleviate the situation, Mrs. Blainey sends the two men away in each other's company. The particularly amusing irony in this turn of events is that Hillingdon is pursued by Muawiya in *A Guest and His Going* much as Perry is in *The Picnic at Sakkara*. Hillingdon's concern with international goodwill causes him at first to take an interest in Muawiya; but after the destruction of his car Hillingdon wants nothing more to do with him. The irony of circumstances also switches these men's positions when Hillingdon becomes at his own home the "chief guest" of Muawiya and the irrepressible Egyptian plays host at the party Perry has arranged for him at Helvetia. Shining with sweat and looking "like a guest of the Borgias," Hillingdon exclaims that the situation is "not natural." "In my own house! . . . You are giving a party in *my* house. It is like being possessed. . . . Can't you see there's more in this than meets the eye?" (90–91).

At this party, Mrs. Blainey, in her gelid English grand manner, lifts the situation, with its opportunity of turning Muawiya in to the police, onto a wider plane than the personal. She assures Muawiya that none of the guests will betray him: "We are all English people here and we all know what the honourable thing is to do, particularly as you've given us such a nice party, and we are your guests and everything. Mind you, if you were a Russian it would be different. I shouldn't hesitate. But when you come to know more about the English you will know that they are specially considerate and courteous to the underprivileged and backward, like yourself, for example" (98–99).

This novel lacks altogether the clarity of theme and purpose of *The Picnic at Sakkara* and even of *Revolution and Roses,* and its structure buckles under the topical political overload. Allegorical implications that so effortlessly emerged in the first novel of the trilogy are now affixed with studied calculation. British exploitation of Egypt is reenacted in the story of Muawiya's fear of exploitation by the national laws and, on the thoroughly private and domestic level, by Mrs. Blainey's exploitation of Hillingdon. Unfortunately, the novel becomes a heterogeneous gathering of stories that are more gratuitously than logically combined. Elaine and Yehia, for example, are present for neither thematic nor narrative purpose, unless her vacillating decision to return with him to Egypt upon his being recalled there is supposed to offer a kind of allegoric view of a newly evolved Anglo-Egyptian relationship: what Perry calls "impersonal necessity" (81). Likewise, the purpose of the Perrys' sexual and marital relationship—they end up sleeping in separate rooms with no hint of ever renewing their intimacy ("it was a long journey, [Perry] thought, out of his wife's bedroom for ever" [242])—is only tenuously related to or influenced by Muawiya's madcap visit, which is the central concern of the novel. To see this development as a reflection of the new Anglo-Egyptian relationship, or of impersonal necessity, is not allegorically feasible; and, like one critic,[9] to regard Muawiya as a "remedy" for the "element of dryness in English life" as depicted in "the gradual civilized but inexorable distancing and formalizing of the relations between Perry and his wife" is to mistake ordinary plot differences for thematic contrast.

Actually, *A Guest and His Going* seems to be a marshaling of themes already inspected elsewhere in the trilogy. Yehia is still caught in the same dilemma of *Revolution and Roses*—having to choose between Elaine and his duty to Egypt. And Muawiya rehearses what *The Picnic at Sakkara* has already presented: "Politics

96                                                        P. H. NEWBY

is one thing, friendship is another. It is well known that England
and Egypt hate each other. That does not mean that you and I hate
each other" (147). The love-hate relationship—private love,
national hate—is thus used for another review.

One new major theme, however, is introduced: the idea of personal responsibility in connection with governmental behavior. This
theme is voiced in a colloquy between the innocent Tim and
Hillingdon, who is on the verge of mental collapse. Tim has been
animadverting upon the government's handling of the Suez
problem, and Hillingdon accuses him of being totally uninformed
about the situation: "No private person," he explains, "knows what
considerations the Government has. Governments know." When
Tim inquires if a man should support the government in whatever it
does, he is answered: "Not in everything, but usually in foreign
policy, because every action is based upon information. . . . We've
got to believe in the goodness of the Government or we should go
mad." But, Tim pursues, if the English behave atrociously,
shouldn't the individual Englishman protest? To which Hillingdon
responds: "There's so much secrecy in public affairs he can't be
sure what he's protesting about. That's what I mean when I say that
unless we believe in the goodness of Government we should go
mad" (154–155). Thus the cultural-political question assumes a
strong color of morality because of Tim's concern.

That Hillingdon is a dabbler in the occult who believes in the
supernatural and claims to have been several times reincarnated
allows the approach to this morality theme to come from a comic
angle. ("Hillingdon was not a Christian but he saw no reason for
not using a Christian hypothesis" [53].) To him the Iron Curtain,
the Cold War, the Berlin Blockade, the Korean War, and Nasser's
nationalization of the Suez Canal can all be explained most profoundly as the workings of some supernatural manipulator, perhaps
the devil. Muawiya, he believes, acts like a man possessed; and he
also has the luck of the devil and a devilish appearance and manner.
"Perhaps the most rewarding way of thinking about Khaslat was as
the Devil himself!" (55). So Hillingdon applies to anything
associated with Muawiya terms like *diabolical, Satanic,* and *hell.*

In one scene toward the end of the novel, Hillingdon sees himself
as being actually tempted by Muawiya, who is seeking forgiveness
for wrecking Hillingdon's car and also begging for his friendship.

This scene evokes in Hillingdon's mind such words as *demonic legions, demonic possession, perdition,* and *sulphur;* and it is written as a parody of Christ's temptation. It occurs on a hilltop where Muawiya offers Hillingdon money and food. " 'Being up on that seat with him,' said Hillingdon, 'it was like being tempted by Satan' " (152).

Certainly the purpose of this episode is not merely to create humor; by the force of the parodic irony, the scene serves as a heuristic comment on the folly of the world through a madman's vision and ultimate role as victim.[10] In the end, institutionalized, Hillingdon says to Perry, "I would give my oath to live the life of a retired and private gentleman. My ambition is broken. Let them have the kingdom!" (220). After the British attack on Egypt, Tim resigns from the Council, an act Perry terms a "silly meaningless" gesture (246). Perry, that "sentimental liberal" and "mild imposter" (26, 28) who is "tired of his own identity" (180), would like to let them have the kingdom too: "But he understood *them* too well. And, in any case, unlike Hillingdon, he knew the kingdom was not his to give" (246).

This novel, and thus the trilogy, ends with Perry's voicing some of Newby's persistent themes. This moderate, tolerant attitude that closes *A Guest and His Going* is the product of Perry's "achieved maturity" in middle age, and an earlier passage in the novel has marked its recognition: "If only one could hold an imaginative balance between what was happening and what was not happening then, surely, one would have achieved maturity. . . . He [Perry] saw now that a man's true stature depended on his ability to hold the actual and the possible in harmony. He might have died at birth. Everything in sight, every breath he took, was a bonus. He climbed the steps at Marble Arch thinking of the moments in history worse than this present Suez crisis" (166–167).

## V   *The Achievement*

*The Picnic at Sakkara* ranks as one of Newby's finest novels and is perhaps the best known of his works; it stands out, as one English reviewer noted, as "an individual achievement."[11] The American edition of the novel was issued with quotations of praise by Evelyn Waugh, V. S. Pritchett, and David Daiches among others; and Daiches has singled it out for brief comment in his survey of modern British literature.[12] The novel has also enjoyed a certain acclaim because of a few quite obvious similarities in theme and situation to Forster's *A Passage to India*, by which Newby was admittedly much influenced.[13] Perhaps most importantly, *The Picnic at Sakkara* established Newby's reputation as a comic writer and has been responsible for his often being placed in the comic tradition in the modern English novel with such predecessors as Forster, Aldous Huxley, Evelyn Waugh, Joyce Cary, and Henry Green and with such a contemporary as Kingsley Amis.[14]

In contrast with the notable success of this novel, the other two novels of the Egyptian trilogy are for several reasons lesser accomplishments. One does not detect behind *Revolution and Roses* and *A Guest and His Going* the kind of impassioned impetus that carries the story of Oliver Knight into a second book. Unlike *The Retreat*, which is so superior an advance beyond *A Step to Silence*, the two later Egyptian novels display a slackening of intensity, a setting of more easily obtained technical goals, and a narrative verbosity absent from the beautifully wrought and economically written *Picnic at Sakkara*.

Each novel is not, however, without its individual interests. *Revolution and Roses* takes the theme of the trilogy and burlesques it as a vain and self-conscious romanticism, and *A Guest and His Going* augments the political theme by means of parody to encompass the moral. But each of these two novels gives the reader a sense of repetition, of material *déjà lu;* and the effectiveness of the morality theme in *A Guest and His Going* is impaired by the odd complexity inherent in the parodic vehicle of its introduction. Furthermore, the contrived situations in these two novels, like those in the comedies of the Restoration, are extremely amusing when read but, because of their very complications, are soon easily forgotten. In *A Guest and His Going*, Muawiya remains a vital comic creation; but the summary treatment of the Perrys deprives them of motivation, lessens their thematic import, and thus turns them into thematic devices who, unable to move about of their own will, must be deployed like counters. Nevertheless, *The Picnic at Sakkara* pulses with life and shows no weakening of beat. And Newby salvages the morality theme of *A Guest and His Going* for a brilliant and entirely successful reworking in *Something to Answer For*.

## CHAPTER 6

# The Middle of the Journey

IN the 1960's, Newby published three novels: *The Barbary Light* (1962), *One of the Founders* (1965), and *Something to Answer For* (1968). The second of these is a short satirical comedy. The other two, which are among his longest and most fully developed novels, tend toward his tragic manner, although *Something to Answer For* comes very close to being the kind of "truly gay book about a desperately tragic situation" that Newby has stated he wants ultimately to write.[1] These two novels are not only among his most outstanding accomplishments but must be ranked among the best English novels of the mid-century.

All three of these novels of the 1960's are concerned with human relationships as seen from the individual, not the social, point of view. Although *One of the Founders* may at first seem to have another primary interest, it nonetheless is typical of Newby's abiding concern with the quest for intangibles. Certain similarities in each of these novels are, in fact, quite noticeable and manifest Newby's practice of reworking related material through several novels in sequence.

Beginning with Perry in *A Guest and His Going*, Newby has concentrated on heroes in middle age, men "in the middle of the journey," as the protagonist says of himself in *One of the Founders* (191). Being at this period of life serves as an important motivation of the men's actions. Each of them is led, like Winter, to make symbolic journeys into the interior of self, journeys which climax in violent moments of revelation and regeneration. In *The Barbary Light* and *Something to Answer For,* the heroes are assaulted, wounded, and stripped—literal acts that carry symbolic thematic significance. In *One of the Founders*, the lesser hero undergoes an equally significant symbolic "baptism" in a dark river. In each instance, the thematic quest is a search for truth, value, and meaning in a world pictured as a wasteland in nightmare.

I   The Barbary Light

*The Barbary Light* is a study of the imagination. The
protagonist, Owen Hanner, is a chartered accountant who collects
debentures. Two events in his childhood were the basis for his sub-
sequent attitudes and behavior. The first of these events resulted in
a disappointment that left him feeling cheated by life. When
twelve years old, he had once gone aboard a freighter and had been
told by the members of the crew that he could sail with them to the
Mediterranean. Imaginative and gullible, he believed the sailors
and also their tale of Barbary pirates. He romantically fancied
himself to be running away to sea, and it was "a peculiarly happy
and meaningful moment for him" (15). But the boat went only into
Cardiff Docks, where it was actually headed with its cargo; and
Owen, "really heartbroken" (25) at having been deceived, was put
ashore.

The second event followed the first immediately. Owen's father
had come to fetch him when he was put off the boat, and on the
way home had told him, "Your mother and I nearly decided not to
have you" (53). The irony of hearing this crushing remark from the
father he was running away from and the ironic outcome of the
episode on the boat proved tragically destructive to the boy's sen-
sibility. He becomes a man unsure of himself and one without a
moral center; now, in middle age, he balances uncertainly between
adultery in his private life and fraud in his professional life.

Owen's "spiritual flowering" (97) becomes the framework of the
plot. Realizing the desolation of his existence, he sees himself as a
"neurotic and self-deceiving, frustrated, haunted victim" (92). He
is a "monster of selfishness" (90) whose self-protective code of conduct is "Hurt or be hurt" (133); he has, he admits, no friends; and
he does not "really communicate" with his wife Sybil (55). His
continuing existence is the result of two "whims"—that of his
parents and that of a German soldier who during the war "could
perfectly well have shot him" but did not (65). Moreover, Owen
hates his job; he "had particularly not wanted to be an accountant," but "his father had made him" (51). Most importantly, he
lacks an identity; he is nothing but a "stand-in character for
himself" (73).

After initiating the sale of the bankrupt business of an elderly

man named Cave, Owen begins, without really consciously knowing why, to start telling the truth; he wants "to confess" and "to
strip himself down to the essentials" (96). He tells his mistress Alex
that he is married; he tells Sybil about Alex. But: "He didn't want
anything to *happen*. He wanted life to go on pretty much as it was.
Perhaps it was unbelievably simple-minded of him but in his drive
for truth he had not, so far, stopped to consider what the consequences of honesty would be. He wanted to be known fully and
understood fully. In return he was prepared to know and understand everybody else fully too" (97).

The plot is developed through a logically related series of conflicting opposites, sometimes symbolic or metaphoric, sometimes
literal. The principal pair in constant struggle is truth and untruth.
A life founded on lies and deceit like Owen's leads to isolation and
solitude, owing in large part to both the failure of communication
and the failure *to* communicate. The composition of such a life is
appearances, not realities; it is disappointments issuing from
romantic illusory expectations, not real fulfillments. Man becomes
an actor; life, a play. Thus the characters' actions are "like im-
provising in a play" (110); and Owen at one point envisions himself
saying to a group of theatergoers, "Applaud *me*. I'm real!" (82).
Cave, too, pursues a course obscuring reality; just as he makes
photographs of clouds, symbols of appearance, so is he blind to the
reality that his bottling company is irredeemably bankrupt. It is a
matter out of which, Owen tells him, he is "just making a drama"
(122). Untruth and isolation altogether diminish man's humanness,
and in the midst of life he leads a cold existence of death.

Sybil first met Owen during a time of snow, which, like clouds, is
a symbol of appearance and anonymity as well as of death; and she
thinks of him as "her snowman" and as one who seems "to come,
or to go, like a god in the clouds" (45). In the early pages of the
novel, Owen and Sybil get lost one night in a snowstorm; and their
struggle to find their way becomes a metaphor of the action of the
whole novel. Owen's remark upon sighting a house, "There's a
light" (42), prefigures the couple's ultimate salvation. The snow
and the night are to give way to the warmth and the light, literal
and symbolic, of the Barbary shore which Owen finds when he at
last arrives there.

Each character's destiny depends on how he exerts and employs

the power of the imagination—a theme of sovereign importance to
Newby. The improper exercise of this faculty has paralyzed the
Hanners' relationship. Sybil wants to be understood but not known
about; people, she believes, "should be left alone, unquestioned,
unexamined" (36). And Owen finds that "something about [her]
. . . had always checked serious, intimate conversation" (55).
Consequently, to ease these tensions, Sybil frequently projects
herself out of the world of reality into a private world of fantasy.
Her first husband Colin, who was killed in the war, returns one
night as a seemingly real presence to Sybil. Thereafter, he often
reappears to her, and they have long conversations. Colin, she
feels, understands her. Sybil, one may say, leads a life of fantastic
bigamy; for her former husband is as real to her as Owen's mistress
is to him. Yet Sybil is paradoxically a widow in both worlds:
whereas Colin is actually dead, Owen is "like a man who hasn't
lived" (122).

When Owen tells his wife about Alex, Sybil is stimulated by this
revelation of truth to take action: she seeks Alex out to tell her that
she will never divorce Owen. When Alex accuses him of being a
contemptible liar, Sybil defends him on the basis of his having no
imagination—one of the principal ironies operative in the Hanners'
marriage.

A subplot works to reveal, among other things, the inaccuracies
of Sybil's imagination. While Owen works in London during the
week, she is employed as a welfare and recruitment officer in a
local factory. A couple of young employees named Pearce, who are
undergoing a crisis in their marriage, are sent to Sybil for advice.
The wife, Fiona, resents the interference and strikes at Sybil on a
vulnerable point: "What d'yer know about girls like me? Yir own
'usband don't live with yir" (26). Sybil's efforts to hold Owen contrast cruelly with her advice to Pearce to divorce his adulterous
wife: "I'd cut my losses if I were you and start again. . . . You've
had a failure. All right, recognize it. Say, 'I've failed.' Don't go on
pretending you haven't failed when you know damn well you've
failed and you're not wanted and just jeered at for not seeing it"
(155–156).

When she first goes to Alex, Sybil finds her ill; and, acting on
compassionate impulse, she arranges for her to recuperate at the
Hanners' house in the Chilterns. Owen is now housed with both his

wife and his mistress in a *ménage à quatre*, the fourth member being the apparitional Colin. The two women become unexpectedly good friends, and Owen is left without the intimacy of either, trapped in a "pattern of almost monastic severity. There was no sex" (124). The humor of the situation is exquisite. Ironically, Sybil's emotional imagination has caught Owen like a force of moral retribution.

It should be emphasized that Newby has seldom before brought characters more convincingly alive. Owen, Sybil, and Alex are unquestionably and engagingly credible, and the events, despite all their overtones of preposterousness, are also believable. What one critic has observed about the action in *The Picnic at Sakkara* is equally applicable here: "This [the action] is delightfully absurd, but the important thing, and the measure of Mr. Newby's curiously insinuating strength as a writer, is that we scarcely realize the absurdity as we read. It seems natural; in a way it *is* natural, in the sense that it is the truth between the lines, the meaning that normally gets left unspoken."[2] The women carry, perhaps, heavy extraliteral burdens. Sybil's name is surely suggestive of her mythic, supernatural qualities (Owen even calls her an elf), and Alex is endowed with boyish physical characteristics as well as with a name that is more often masculine than feminine. Sybil is fair and Alex is dark like the good and bad ladies of the romance tradition. But they carry these burdens lightly and easily, and they move gracefully and freely outside the reservation of stock expectation.

Alex, for instance, is not to be a villainess; her imagination prevents her being so. Like Sybil, she has been deceived by Owen; but, also like Sybil, she loves him and does not want to give him up. During Alex's convalescence at the Hanners' home in the country, her self-understanding develops simultaneously with her awareness of Sybil's "seriousness and generosity," so that Sybil's "magnanimity" turns the otherwise farcical situation into "a matter for heart-searching" (148). Alex's fate is ironic: imagination causes her to give up what she wants because she cannot be what she would like to be, as she tells Sybil: "I'd like to be the complete bitch. I've got the right instincts. Having taken as much from you as I can I'd really like to depart with Owen tied to my chariot wheel. In theory I can see how splendid this would be. In practice I haven't got the character. Like most mean-minded people I'm a

coward. Once having taken Owen away from you I'd be waiting for
my reward, some other woman taking him away from me" (152).
Thus her imaginative awareness and her appreciation of Sybil's
good qualities cause Alex to renounce Own and leave. The instrument of good, triumphing over its opposite, is the imagination.

Alex's imagination brings insight into herself and others, but
Cave's imagination is a source of self-delusion (as Sybil's often is).
The elderly man thinks Owen is deliberately ruining him, but Cave
in reality is a victim of himself; he is enervated by an overactive,
uncontrolled imagination. A man alone, he has been only inter-
mittently an inhabitant of the factual world. After the loss of his
company, he transfers the blame to Owen and is unutterably happy: "The winding up of his business was what he had been secret-
ly yearning for all these years" (229). He is glad to be rid of any
reminder of his failure, and he is enthusiastically making a
photographic record of the building of a new factory on the old
site. "It's a change from clouds," he says (229); but the change is,
significantly, not so marked as he thinks, since this new fascination
denotes his habitual preoccupation with unreality. As he explains,
the lighting in the factory will be artificial: "It's the modern thing.
You can't rely on natural light" (228).

Owen's attitude toward Cave is complex. He sees him as a victim
of modern industrialization, as an incompetent businessman, as a
fatherly figure (even a father-surrogate), and as a moral scold. Being both attracted to and repelled by Cave, Owen is yet another instance in Newby's fiction of the man who is confused by the contradictions and disharmonies that exist between the public and
private aspects of his life. Professionally, Owen is selling Cave out;
personally, he responds to him warmly, compassionately, wistfully,
wishfully. From the first, Cave has caused in Owen "a stirring and
an articulation of the consciousness" (72); therefore, Cave can exert
a decisive influence upon him.

Notwithstanding the fact that Cave never attains a true glimpse
of himself, he is spasmodically capable of imaginatively detecting
truth behind deceit, realities behind appearances, patterns within
amorphousness. Speaking from his unguarded heart, the elder man
alerts the younger to the desiccative effects of a duplicitous existence. He reproves Owen from his own moral position, and he ad-
monishes him to acquire the virtues of a practicing im-

agination—which he ably defines in Newby's terms: "You've got to put yourself into other people's position. Half the trouble of the world would be avoided if people were to do that. Not just understanding somebody else's point of view. I mean *being* them. Being your poor wife. Or me, for example. . . . One day you'll understand what I mean. Then you'll give up this dreadful work" (128).

Owen's spiritual flowering results from his coming to grips with the imagination, through hard self-scrutiny, as a formative principle and code of living. His situation has become a morass of confusion, private and public. In addition to the difficulties with wife and mistress, not solved by Alex's departure because Sybil believes that Owen still wants Alex, he has been notified that he must appear before a disciplinary investigative committee for professional malpractice in connection with Cave's factory. Because Owen has sold Cave's property to a company he himself controls through nominees and has then resold it at a profit, he is likely to lose his certification. At this point, he has to reconnoiter and prepare to begin all over again; and the narrative now follows the mythic pattern of departure-absence-return. In the second of these three stages, Owen as hero will go through an experience that will yield him a transforming illumination and enable him to return readjusted, a whole man capable of constructive and effective action. Like the imagination, the mythic experience will serve to define the hero's identity and to gather him into the harmonic sweetness of common humanity.

Owen's journey—the psychological and mythic as well as the literal, for they become one and the same—is thus the climax of the novel. He travels to Africa alone, making at last the trip which as a boy he had not made: "What a man had done once he could do again" (21). This trip beautifully shapes the narrative into a significant symmetry of balanced opposites. Owen's plan to sail to Africa with the sailors on the freighter "was a hell of a decision to take" (18); and, going there in middle age, he finds Tunis "a hell of a disappointment" (253). What is important, as well as relevant to Owen's growth of character, is that his romantic illusion has given way to reality, recognized and admitted. This admission of failure frees him from self-deception; it indicates an exit from unreality, a winning of truth, and (in Sybil's words) the beginning of wisdom.

Thoroughly isolated as a stranger in a foreign place, Owen suffers physical violence when he is attacked, robbed, and wounded in one eye. The attack, robbery, and wounding are different only in their physical nature from those he had incurred during, and as a result of, the escapade in his youth. But this time "Owen felt he had received punishment he had deserved" (242), for his present ordeal is an expiation and a purgation that culminate in spiritual rebirth. When he returns, he is "like a man raised from the dead" (215), as were those other mythic travelers, Winter and Knight; he is no longer the "old Hanner" but the "new one" (250).

Owen gains, first of all, knowledge of himself: "You went down into darkness to see what was invisible in sunlight" (260). Swimming naked in the warm dark sea, at last stripped "down to the essentials" and to the unlaughable nakedness of humanity, he watches the flashing Carthage light as if it were sending him a message: "He no longer supposed he'd been the victim of any deliberate cheat in his life" (219); indeed, the only pirate he finds in Barbary is himself. Furthermore, he acquires insight into a meaning for life; and the removal of his eye-patch when his wound has improved is a symbolic device, the physical change indicating outwardly the spiritual change. The trip thus provides restoration, and a new insight is the reward of the quest.

This new insight is founded on the imagination. "Shocked into an ugly sense of reality" (248), Owen realizes that "this precisely was what it meant to be human: to have illusions," that "life was something you were intended to imagine" (252). As a child, Owen had lost his illusions or had been robbed of them. With that loss had occurred also a loss of humanness and communion, and Owen had been reduced to a lower level. As a "sublunary man" subject to "change, chance and decay" (189), he has fallen from the human to the animal level—a point sharpened by the numerous animal images associated with Owen. All his life he has "been in thwarted flight from the present into the larger freedom where mere objects, sensations, hopes, boots, dreams, grass, questionings, were never-endingly washed by some sustaining tide of understanding" (246). He, the sublunary man, has desired to ascend to the translunar eternal moment—"Up to that region beyond the moon where there was a stainless and unchanging reality" (189); but, thus far, he has not been able to bridge the discrepancy between appearance and reality or to sustain the shock of disillusionment. Now, however, he formulates as a guiding principle for living the idea that appearance can be *made* reality through the exertion and exercise of the synthesizing imagination, that uniquely human faculty: this concept will end the solitude of his existence and recover his lost happiness. For him, reality has been solitude; it was, in his own figure of speech, a pit that, animal-like, he has had to climb out of.

Directed by the "larger illumination" (219) that he had gone to Africa to seek, Owen returns to England, to Sybil, and to a new reality; he is "eager to see, now, how much reality he could put up with" (257). His reassuring reunion with Sybil vanquishes Colin: "He wasn't a real presence [to her] any more. He could not be summoned" (280). Moreover, Sybil tempers her own imagination which, having been carried to an extreme degree, had become harmful. It had become fantasy, productive of self-torment, sentimentality, distortion of personality: in short, falsity. And falseness cuts one off, isolates one, unlike the controlled imagination, which is a moral good because it binds men together.

Now prepared to face the consequence of the practice of fraud even though "it'll be thumbs down" (286), Owen reiterates with conviction the talismanic idea that he has brought back with him from Carthage: "Imagination. Life was what you imagined it to be" (265). No better tonic, apparently, can be found for the ailing modern man and woman whom Owen and Sybil represent; for "their malaise," says Newby, "is spiritual" (273).

## II One of the Founders

*One of the Founders* comes between *The Barbary Light* and *Something to Answer For* like a satirical scherzo. It is composed of two plots. One deals with the private man; the other, with the public man. The protagonist of both plots is Ian Hedges, a thirty-nine-year-old Borough Education Officer who is "a slightly thyroid, incipient manic-depressive, heterosexual, and . . . lapsed Anglican" (191). As Ian ("Jack"), he is a kind of representative Englishman of the modern welfare state; and the name may be a device to alert the reader that the novel in hand is allegorical.

However that may be, Ian's surname, Hedges, is clearly referential.
He is

> a man like any other man: the son of the town butcher, backward at his
> elementary school because of asthma; a conscientious objector for the first
> six months of the war (then he changed his mind); a good teacher during
> the three years he had in the schools (he saw no reason to conceal his good
> points); a useful fly-half until four years ago, when he had broken his leg;
> fond of dancing and traditional jazz; an irrational supporter of Newcastle
> United (irrational because he had never been to Newcastle, never seen the
> team play, was not interested in soccer as a game, but stayed at home on
> Saturday evening until he knew whether they had lost or won); an oc-
> casional, but pusillanimous, gambler on the Stock Exchange; the possessor
> of a Scottish Christian name because his mother (cook in the household of
> local gentry) had come from Dumfries. And he had been a cuckold.
> (17—18)

Ian's wife Nell has divorced him and married a journalist named
Brush, a "hanger-on, drunkard, and adulterer" (38). Hedges, hedg-
ing, is still fond of Nell and is concerned about her happiness; he
sends her birthday cards and lends money to Brush.

When Ian meets Prudence Styles, a teacher, he responds daring-
ly to her obvious beauty. But, when he tries to kiss her, she stabs
him in the foot with the stiletto heel of her shoe. Wounded but un-
discouraged, he continues to pursue her. She becomes pregnant by
him; but, being prudently imprudent, she refuses to marry him:
"She did not believe that marriage should be based on an accidental conception" (173). Nell, grown jealous, tries unsuccessfully to
get Hedges back; she then abandons Brush for Gideon Toplis (of
Toplis Mouldings), a local magnate. Hedges nearly kills the
drunken Brush in a ludicrous sword fight by thrusting him in the
throat, but the poor fellow recovers, although he has lost his voice,
and goes to live abroad. Still chasing Prudence, Hedges has a noc-
turnal "Experience" on a freezing river, an experience that, after
his plunge into the dark water, results in self-revelations about
"what it was to be human" (249). Finally, old Mr. Hedges, Ian's
father, falls ill; and, on the night when he dies, Prudence moves in
with Ian and agrees to marry him.

Intertwined with this plot of private human relations is the plot
of public relations. Hedges learns from Prudence that her father,

who lives in nearby Brewchester, is engaged in an effort to have a university established there; and Hedges wonders why his own native town, Perstowe, should not have a university. He starts a campaign; a promotion committee is formed; a group, including Hedges, seeks the assistance of a townsman's friend in the Treasury; competition with Brewchester for the university flares up, since obviously only one of the closely situated towns will be selected; a fund drive is organized; Hedges resigns from the committee; and, at last, Perstowe is granted the university.

The attempt to unify the two plots into a significant form indicates Newby's continual technical experimentation; but, while that attempt itself is praiseworthy, its success is notably qualified. The novel that results seems a collaboration between the two kinds of modern novelists that Newby has identified, the historian and the poet. The heart of the novel is the plot about Hedges's private life; and it is the work of the poet, or mythmaker, who is occupied with universals. Enclosing that plot is the one about the university, which is the work of the historian, who is concerned with particulars and committed to contemporary topics and issues (" 'live' issues and 'contemporary' themes, too fresh and unfermented for distilling into art but lending themselves to a kind of imaginative reportage," according to Honor Tracy in her review of *One of the Founders*).[3]

What happens is that this novel fails to cohere because each of the two plots has a distinctively individual tone; and these tones are in constant disharmony because of the different manner in which each plot is treated. The private plot is characteristic of Newby's work in that it is basically mythic. Hedges, the hero in search of transcendental values, is the uncertain man in quest of absolutes and of a unified, decisive personality. This plot Newby treats in a fundamentally somber tone; this small man with large problems, in spite of his frivolous actions, Newby views as worthy of respect, concern, compassion. Sympathetic imagination impels earnest seriousness; therefore, while comicalities of action divert in the foreground, Hedges is presented as unobtrusively developing as a dynamic character in the background.

The public plot, contrastingly, develops as satire, for which Newby's penchant and talent first projected themselves, spottily, in the Egyptian trilogy. The humor and wit are directed against the public man and the grand public action which, as Newby demonstrates, are too foolish to warrant anything but unmasking, deflating, and general ridicule. Thus Hedges the hero is placed in a milieu of fools, and the greater fool he when he consorts with them.

The overall impression is that Newby was more intrigued by and concerned with the satirical than with the mythical plot, and quite the best aspect of the novel lies in his satirical devices. The narrative is set with scintillant epigrams—"Idealism is all right . . . provided you're serving your own interests at the same time" (94); "Scandal is an important social cohesive" (179); "A bit of inflated idealism turns out to be rooted in somebody's disease" (269). Numerous topics are conversed upon, in the fashion of Aldous Huxley's novels. The following are examples: education—"When a university isn't teaching its students to be doctors, scientists, teachers, lawyers, and parsons, that is precisely the function I expect of it, to induce a suspension of disbelief over as wide an area as possible" (29–30); communications—"You, Hedges, believe in truth with a capital T. You believe that this truth has been revealed. You believe that the press and the mass media are the channels through which unsullied truth should pour" (40); religion—"the modern Protestant theologian believes so little nowadays there's very little *doctrinal* reason why everybody shouldn't be Christian" (76–77); government—"People who labour in a bureaucracy have one governing thought: the avoidance of work. This is the obsession of Whitehall. . . . Only by impartiality and justice can Government avoid labour into the small hours" (124–125); civil employees—"He's said something that, without being actually irrelevant, leaves him uncommitted, and what more could a Civil Servant ask?" (135); sex—"Sex is what is known as a consummatory situation. That is what [she and I] did last August. We consummated" (230).

This novel also contains the torrential catalogue, such as the description of Hedges already quoted, whimpering out on a note of anticlimax ("And he had been a cuckold"), or the description of the Long Gallery of Lack Park manor:

[This] was the finest feature of the house, though the pictures that had once hung there had long ago been sold to pay death-duties. The Pigges had been great hunters and travellers; they had placed the usual antlers, tusks, horns, heads, and weapons on the walls, and, as they had little market value, there the relics still hung—tiger, eland, buffalo, boar—gazing down at the silver urns, the china, the white table-cloths. There were huge, stuffed pike in glass cases, crossed spears, rosettes of scimitars and axes. Etc. (183)

Characters have funny names and constitute a collection of grotesques. The plot runs toward the farcical, the inconsequential episode. Large gatherings occur and are ruled by confusion and chaos. And the diction includes frank crudities and vulgarities. All these satirical devices are quite new in Newby's fiction.

Like almost all of Newby's heroes, whether great or small, Hedges undergoes a series of violently decisive experiences. But these particular experiences, so important in Hedges's development, come about either gratuitously or unexpectedly; they are, therefore, incidental to the line of action which Hedges himself is pursuing or planning. For all of their effect on him, the sword fight with Brush and Hedges's initiatory fall into the river impinge upon, instead of developing out of, that action; and the death of old Mr. Hedges is actually extraneous to it. Ian has two main concerns, founding a university and obtaining Prudence; and he sees some kind of redemption or resurrection in these two acts; but the university project soon becomes irrelevant, just as does Hedges's persistent courting of Prudence. That is, he withdraws from the former, and Prudence finally accepts him in spite of, not because of, his courtship.

The idea motivating Hedges is that "as many people as possible . . . [should get] to know each other *personally*," a situation upon which "a happy society" absolutely depends (16, 17). Taking pride in *not* living "the unexamined life" (56), he is actually aware of his lack of self-knowledge and is dominated by the "anybody-can-kick-my-behind feeling" (55). Living a life of lies and delusions, he craves a life of truth and openness.

Hedges's emotional paralysis has resulted from his wife's desertion and divorce and her marriage to the contemptible Brush, who has cuckolded him. Hedges has been stripped, in this event, of both private life and personal identity. He seeks to compensate through the substitution of public act: "Basically, that's why I thought up the university project. I'm the type who's never fully

himself until he's got a cause" (54). But Prudence, whom *he* accuses of immaturity and lack of self-knowledge, dazes him with the
truth that he does not know about himself: "Everything you do is
done to distract you from the fact of being alive," she tells him
(169).

Up to this point, Hedges has been an egregious dunce; and the
topical satire directed against numerous public institutions and
attitudes also scores him. The pseudo-allegorical and mythical
elements, to the confounding of effect, come into play only as self-
mockers. The romance of Hedges and Prudence is styled—rather
arbitrarily since she, not he, is the dominant person in the
relationship—as an affair in terms of the story of Sleeping Beauty.
Prudence's landlady, Mrs. Kidwelly, who lives on top of Mythe
Hill, is dubbed (to no clear purpose) "the fair Medusa" (109) and is
endowed with the power of "her stare" to kill "stone dead" (113).

A more serious element is incorporated when the university, at
Hedges's insistence, must be conceived of as the New Jerusalem;
and Hedges, already a metaphorical prince, becomes, functionally,
a quixotic Crusader. Coalescing Christian and Classical mythical
ritual, Newby has Hedges, self-consciously and knowingly, posit
the requirement of a sacrificial victim. This role falls to Brush,
whom Hedges nearly kills with a cavalry sword. Hedges perceives
Brush as "the bull-headed monster" and supposes that "Theseus
must have felt very much as he [Hedges] did before knocking off
the Minotaur" (198). The whole scene to Hedges is one in which
he "could see himself bathing in and drinking the blood of the
magic animal"; indeed, opening an artery in Brush's body would
be like releasing "a fountain of life" (197). The submerged motive,
personal revenge against the lustful man who took Hedges's wife
away from him, becomes a submerged satirical pun upon the concept of capric Brush as a scapegoat. Myth can of course be used
comically and satirically, but in this novel the very mythic foundation which supports the hero's saving experience and thereby gives
meaning to the action is simultaneously employed as a device of
critical disparagement. The creative process of Newby, who desires
to achieve multivaried effects, is seriously faulty in *One of the
Founders;* and the fault is much more serious than the mere
"miscalculation" that Anthony West remarked upon in his review
of the novel.[4]

As a result of this confusion, or mismatching, of methods—one not unlike that in *A Season in England*—*One of the Founders* fails on almost every level to convince. Hedges's exaltation after the fight with Brush; his having "been purged, transfigured, and lifted up" (208); his misadventure on the river, a parody of the archetypal night-sea journey—these episodes ring false and seem too persistently contrived. Ironically, Newby's prodigal artifice corresponds to Hedges's own lavish self-distractions.

The novel, presumably, dramatizes and satirizes the conflicts and disorders that ensue when one adheres exclusively to opposing extremes. These are specified as man as "political animal" (119) and man as "religious animal" (228). The public life of the political animal warps (at the best) or destroys (at the worst) the integrity of personality. In Hedges's case, the public act—though meant to lead to self-discovery and to be an authentication of selfhood itself—functions paradoxically to distract him from "the fact of being alive." As Anthony West discerned, Newby is here dealing with the idea that "people are real when they are true to themselves in their inner lives and unreal when they are fulfilling their roles in a modern society."[5] With Prudence's assistance, Hedges finally realizes this fact "in the middle of the journey, in the middle of [his life]" (191); and, having progressed from an illusory (and delusory) innocence to a tardy maturity of experience, he sees life as more than "making a series of derisive and contemptuous gestures" (55).

Too extreme a devotion to the role of religious animal also leads to false poses and becomes what Hedges calls a "displacement-activity" (227), a self-denying practice of using ineffective substitutes for the vitalizing real thing. Just as the project of the university was a deceptive public form of attaining salvation of the self, symbolized as the New Jerusalem, but was in reality only Hedges's way of "preening himself" (227) and of compensating for the loss of his wife, so the mawkishly altruistic, masochistic caretaking of his divorced wife and her new husband is a form of self-discredit or self-displacement. Since Hedges lacks the "ability to loathe," he is but half a man; to acquire this "essential biological mechanism" is to be more than "half alive" (138). Again, paradoxically, learning to loathe produces simultaneously the ability to love.

As a satirist, Newby establishes a norm between these two extremes by allowing Hedges to steer a mid-course between political and religious shores. The norm advocated is, quite simply, the personal relationship founded on love mutually offered and mutually accepted. This ideal relationship creates through marriage, for the man and woman together and individually, what it naturally defines—an identity at once public and private. Says Hedges: "I've been scoured, brain-washed, raped, exorcized, given the whole bloody treatment. Of the few natural, good, and meaningful acts of my life, there is one only that still has a glow on it, and that is what Prudence and I did on the floor of her father's sitting room last August. Everything else in my life is a farce and a mockery. This one act is what my life has been for. If this idiot of a girl [Prudence] would marry me, I should know why God created heaven and earth" (236).

Allegorically, Hedges represents the ordinary sensitive citizen in perplexity in the present-day socialist state. The overriding public control and public concern have robbed Jack of his individuality, his identity, his privacy; and fundamental relationships have lost their definition. Who can say, the allegory insistently queries, "I'm all right, Jack"? Hedges himself can say so with qualifications, in the end, after a tortuous journey through not only the interior but also the exterior world. The skeptical novelist, still parodying, does not, however, end the novel in such an unguarded position. Hedges, Prudence, and their newborn child, he says, still mixing methods, "all lived more or less happily for quite a long time after" (285).

## III   Something to Answer For

At the center of *Something to Answer For* [6] is the Suez Canal crisis of 1956; but, despite its importance, it is not the central subject. The novel, as Newby himself has declared, is primarily about morality, not politics.[7] The Suez Canal situation is the backdrop and the magnified parallel to the adventures of the hero, Jack Townrow; it is also the ingenious device that functions to project the hero's situation onto a plane of universal significance. Such a paralleling of the private and the public worlds is not new in Newby's fiction, since he first used it in the Oliver Knight novels, again in *The Picnic at Sakkara,* and, in a rather strained manner, in *A Guest and His Going.* In this latest novel, extraordinary originality and rich complexity are manipulated with the ease and confidence of the artist who has complete mastery of his art: *Something to Answer For* is a thoroughly achieved, tightly integrated work of art.[8]

Technically and thematically, Townrow dominates the novel. He is the most complex, the most interesting, the most vital, and withal the most engaging protagonist yet created in Newby's novels. Like his immediate predecessors—Perry, Owen, Hedges—he is a man in middle age, exactly in the "middle of the journey"; like all of Newby's principal characters, he is bewildered; but, unlike all the others, with the sole exception of Muawiya, he is a cocky, clever, self-sufficient man of action.[9] And the reader knows an enormous amount about Townrow, even down to physical particulars: he is drawn with a true Jamesian "solidity of specification."

The reader learns about John Farrer Townrow "in strips and patches," which is how Townrow himself says he sees his life (209). By his own admission, he is a handsome man—"I am golden" (82). His manner of living is hedonistic: "He liked nice things: food, clothes, drink, women. The main thing was to . . . *enjoy* yourself" (19). And, though he occasionally admits to being a crook, but in flattering terms ("although I'm a crook I'm untouched by sin" [138]), he readily confesses to having "spasms of dishonesty, lechery and disloyalty" (81). Born on November 2, Townrow has characteristics considered typical of a Scorpio subject. Ruled by Mars, he is secretive, energetic, determined, passionate; for him, sex, as well as religion, can be a strong motivating force. One of his mistresses, a Capricorn subject and a reader of books on astrology, contrasts herself with him: " 'I know where I'm going,' she had said. 'I'm ruled by my head. I'm not like you, emotional. . . . I'm mature. I never do things on impulse' " (272).

When Townrow was a child, his father deserted his mother; impulsively during a ride in the country, he had got out of the car, had set off across a field, and had never returned. Townrow's Irish mother, a teacher, reared him. "She brainwashed me," he says (191); "Crazy old bitch, really" (190). He attended a theological college; but in March, 1942, he was expelled (a girl had falsely accused him of getting her pregnant), went into the army, and turned atheist. In 1946, he was a sergeant waiting to be "demobbed" at Port Said when he had an accident: he fell on his head outside the

beach hut of Elie Khoury and his English wife Ethel, who befriend-
ed him. Townrow married and divorced a woman named Jean and
had an affair with one called Liz. Now, in the summer of 1956, he
is doing quite well. He is no longer paying alimony and is prosper-
ing because he is embezzling a disaster fund of which he is the dis-
tributor.

At this point in Townrow's life, the narrative proper of
*Something to Answer For* opens. Elie Khoury has recently died,
and Mrs. Khoury—"a shrewd, practical, hard old trot" (12)—has
asked Townrow to come to Egypt and help her settle affairs. Since
she is rich and without heirs, Townrow begins "to see himself as
[her] sole beneficiary" (11) and accepts. On the night of his arrival
in Port Said, he is attacked—smashed on the head, stripped, and
abandoned in the desert. Thereafter, mentally confused and partially amnesiac, he is certain about nothing, not even his own identity and nationality.

He soon becomes the lover of Leah Strauss, daughter of Abravanel, Mrs. Khoury's Jewish lawyer. As the affair continues, Townrow begins to think that he may be Leah's American husband,
who is in Cleveland undergoing mental treatment. He also believes
that he is Irish and urges Mrs. Khoury to put her Egyptian holdings
in his name and go to England. The Egyptians, he tells her, would
not sequester the estate of an Irishman; but she slyly refuses to take
this advice. She has never liked the Irish, she says; they "are un-
trustworthy and they tell lies and they drink" (94).

During a mob attack on Mrs. Khoury's apartment, Townrow kills
one of the rioters and his situation in Port Said grows more complicated and more precarious. Now suspected of murder, he is also
believed to be a Jew and (by both the police and a ring of
smugglers) a spy and a secret agent. He feels that he must get
away—"He needed a bit of security. The time had come to cut his
losses" (119)—and he takes a steamer one night across Lake Man-
zala for an island that belonged to Elie. When the steamer runs
aground in the middle of the lake, Townrow lowers a dinghy into
the water and makes for shore by himself. He decides to obtain
food and water, then to sail out into the open sea, and to hail a boat
going to Europe. Instead, he spends several days on the lake and
finally comes to shore in bad shape. There an old man cares for
him, and he lives on a bench beside a saint's tomb. After a long

stay, he decides he must return to Port Said to clear up matters, at least in his own head.

He arrives just when the Egyptians, in control of the Suez Canal, are to permit a convoy through it for the first time. To all the Europeans' surprise, and to Townrow's immense delight, the Egyptians succeed—and on schedule. Soon afterwards, the British start bombings; and Townrow and Leah are arrested. He is interrogated by a military tribunal and put on a train for Cairo, but during an air attack he manages to escape.

Leah has been released, and Townrow finds her at her apartment with her father, who is dying. She is preparing to leave the country. In order to persuade Mrs. Khoury to leave Port Said, which is under attack, Townrow has Elie's body exhumed. He sees that Leah's father is buried and, three days later, takes Leah, Mrs. Khoury, and Elie's body, after considerable trouble, in a small boat to a British warship that will give them passage. Townrow himself refuses to board, remains in the small boat, and drifts out to the open sea. He is "setting a course for some point near the heart," having "decided, absolutely, to answer for himself," alone (283, 284).

This elaborate plot (of which many intricacies have been omitted) is really concerned with one action—the moral change in Townrow.[10] The narrative shows how, as the result of a change of outlook, he replaces a standard of behavior based on dishonesty and dishonor with a standard based on the exactly opposite principles. In making this about-face, he moves from bondage, especially to money and women, to a complete and temerarious sense of freedom. Newby has described his conception of the novel in this way: "What interested me was the situation of a man who was a rogue; an Englishman, who nevertheless assumed, as many English people do, that by and large the society he lives in is governed by good forces—forces that are operating wisely and well. . . . So I wondered what would happen to a rogue who suddenly in an unmistakable way had to confront the possibility that the centre of power in his own society was as corrupt as he was himself."[11] Townrow, being in Port Said at a time of international crisis, "would naturally go through a process of questioning about the rightness or wrongness of his government," and the personal crisis would thus be caused by and concomitant with the international. In the end, Townrow finds that the way of nations offers him no valid, dependable standard; and, says Newby, he arrives at "a situation in which he realises that it's very hard for the individual to answer for anything but the state of his own conscience."

Because this experience takes place in a period of less than six months, Newby was much concerned to make the rapid cycle of the change in Townrow "plausible and utterly convincing." He decided that, to succeed, there must be a form of "physical intervention," and for this reason he introduced the hit on Townrow's head to make the "complexity and strangeness" of the novel "susceptible of a perfectly naturalistic, scientific explanation." The head-blow also served Newby, however, in yet another way, which he has commented upon. He "wanted to involve the reader in the situation with Townrow as much as [he] could," and he could do so "by subjecting the reader to a certain amount of surprise and uncertainty himself—so that he could rub his eyes and go back and say did he mean that, or so and so." Thus the "mystification" and "complication" do not exist in the novel for just their own sake but as a device to make reading the novel, like the novel itself, an involved, unifying experience.

The reader's difficulty—what makes him "rub his eyes" and forces him to stay continuously alert—is keeping straight, and deciding the actuality of, at least four levels of reality. The point of view is occasionally omniscient, thus helping the reader at certain places (for example, one reads that Townrow "was so taken up with this sudden flood of clear recollection" [190]); but it is usually limited to Townrow, whose mind has "skidded" (47) and whose brain is "bent" (42). These two levels of reality, the objective and the subjective, alternate with two others, dreams and lies. Townrow is subject to dream sequences; and, because his dreams are so vivid, he cannot separate them from reality or even sort them out chronologically. Though not "half in love with easeful death," he may well ask, "Do I wake or sleep?" And yet, if he wakes, he cannot be trusted to tell the truth: "I'm a good liar," he boasts (63). Furthermore, his very livelihood is based on the skillful juggling of appearance and reality. Thus consciously and unconsciously he interchanges fact and fiction, reality and imagination, truth and lies; and he also assumes various disguises and plays various roles. A man both spatially and temporally disconnected, he often feels "ex-

hausted by the effort of hanging on to the real world. He had to
relax only for one moment and he was caught up in dreams and
fantasies" (117). Consequently, "You honestly did not know who
you were or what you were doing" (170).

The structure of the novel is as intricate as the two narrative
points of view and the oscillating levels of reality. The main line of
events progresses in a generally straightforward manner: Townrow
goes to Egypt, encounters a variety of people and experiences, and
leaves. But, since the story of Townrow coincides with the Suez
crisis, the novel actually traces, and develops, the two series of
events—the private-fictional and the public-historical—simultaneously. In addition, because of Townrow's mental condition,
some events involving him (past? present? future? real? true?
dream?) are fragmented and scattered about out of time and out of
order.

Finally, in the concluding chapter of the novel, Newby narrates
two major episodes together in alternating pieces rather than se-
quentially. One of these is the burial of Abravanel, which has just
taken place; the other is Townrow's transporting Leah, Mrs. Khoury, and the corpse of Elie out of the harbor. Each event moves
forward in time together with the other, first this one, then that;
but, temporally, the reader is tracking at once a series of events occurring in time past and a series of events occurring in time present. The complexity, however, does not stop here. One of Townrow's dreams that repeatedly recurs hauntingly in his unbolted
memory, and that is mentioned in the first paragraph of the novel,
is "that Mrs. Khoury, Mr. Khoury and he were all sailing out of the
harbour in a boat that slowly filled with water."

This dream, as the novel proceeds, becomes confused with a
sometimes varied tale about the dead Elie's having already been
taken out of the harbor with a wildly elaborate deception and carried to Lebanon. In one version of the dream, Mrs. Khoury takes
him by herself; in another, Christou, a barman, disguised as a woman, takes the corpse away. The dream becomes, therefore, a
steadily expanding, mutating motif; finally, it becomes reality:
"The experience was too much like a dream. You hated it but you
could not wake up" (271); "At best [Townrow] could say the dream
or some obscure recollection put this particular trip into his mind"
(277); "Townrow was breaking into his dream. He had been here

before" (280); and "The experience was not quite as he remembered it. . . . But essentially it was the same dream he had climbed back into" (281). Townrow is back where he started, *temporally;* the present is ending, but it is also starting again, back in the past.

The structure of *Something to Answer For* is an almost perfect balance, for it divides into two halves that are repetitive to a degree but are clearly contrasting. The first half ends with Townrow's experience on the lake with the original plan of sailing out to sea in the dinghy. The second half begins, like the other, with his entrance into Port Said and, also like the first half, ends with Townrow's setting out to sea in a small boat.[12] The contrast stems from Townrow's change: he returns from the lake after a symbolic death and rebirth as a different person, "a good man" (132). In the first half, Townrow realizes: "The hell of being among strangers was that nobody formed any expectation of how you would behave; therefore you did not know how to behave. You had no notion of what your appropriate conduct would be. You did not know whether you were good, bad or indifferent" (71). In the second half, he can proclaim: "I'm saved" (132). The baffling and mysterious problems raised and encountered in the first half are met head-on and either solved or abandoned in the second.

Such a structure is contrapuntal. The second half of the novel inverts the first half, point for point. Moreover, themes (or events) are developed in a contrapuntal fashion that is, appropriately, fugal; and the final chapter bears a remarkable resemblance to *stretto,* the contrapuntal technique, commonly used in final sections of musical fugues, by which themes occur in close succession and overlap—the purpose being to create climactic intensity. Moreover, the final chapter of *Something to Answer For,* the title of which interestingly incorporates the musical formal term "A Sea Requiem," can be also viewed as a nonfugal *stretto;* that is, a concluding section of a musical composition in an accelerated tempo.

The fugal technique is doubly appropriate in this novel since *fugue (fuga)* is literally "flight" and since the plot of *Something to Answer For* is, in thematic terms, a series of flights (beginning with a flight by air; ending with one by water) that are engaged in by a man who can state that "he was on the move. That was what he liked. Pressing forward. He liked new scenes, new faces, new experiences. A man who stayed put was in decay. You stepped on a plane [as he has already done] or a boat [as he will do] and before you knew where you were some new game was being explored. You fell into some new relationship and you became a different person" (121–122). Second, *fugue* as a psychiatric term defines "a period during which a patient suffers from loss of memory and often begins a new life";[13] in this sense, *fugue* is singularly apt as a description of Townrow's Egyptian experiences, at the conclusion of which he announces, "I've been a sick man. I'm O.K. now" (264).

The texture of the novel is, then, contrapuntal; it is a composition of quests in fugue. These enter one at a time, in fugal fashion, and grow into intricate complexities, often unforeseen, as they develop and overlap. There are at least five quests; first is Townrow's single-minded, knavish quest for tangibles—money, then women. He goes to Egypt to obtain for himself as much of Mrs. Khoury's fortune as he can; and, as an experienced grafter and dishonest manipulator of money for his own gain, he views the prospects for his chicanery as brightly promising. And he loses no time, once in Port Said, in establishing a sexual relationship with Leah. But the quest does not proceed either so patly or so smoothly as he has anticipated. On the one hand, Mrs. Khoury—"tough" and possessed of "the courage of some half-mad old pussycat run wild" (169)—is skeptical of his actions, intentions, and suggestions; on the other hand, Leah is quick to perceive that Townrow is "obviously on the make, in more ways than one" (83). This quest becomes, in the end, a failure; a *salutary* failure. Not only does Townrow give up Leah but he writes his will and gives "all [his] real estate, goods, chattels and other possessions, including the gold ring on [his] finger, in Port Said" to Mrs. Khoury and all his "property and possessions in the United Kingdom" to Leah's mad husband (244, 246). Loss of tangible possessions will free Townrow to take on intangible replacements.

Mrs. Khoury has told Townrow that her husband did not die a natural death but was, she is convinced, murdered; and from this situtation the second quest evolves. Townrow's inquiries about where Elie is buried lead to conflicting answers, and he begins a search for the man's body. When Mrs. Khoury herself claims to have just seen her husband alive, the search for a corpse becomes a search for a living man. Townrow himself, under the influence of Mrs. Khoury's claim and his own dreams and hallucinated condition, thinks he too sees Elie. Once Townrow talks to him; another time, he runs after him on the streets.

This quest, apart from providing diverting suspenseful action similar to that in a thriller, is significant because of the contrast it provides, as a minor diversion, to the major quest of the novel: Townrow's search for himself, his own identity. An attack on his self-confidence is begun in the Rome airport during his trip out to Port Said when a group of traveling foreigners assail him with questions about the rectitude and integrity of the English national character. Says one to him: "[The Englishman] thinks he is good and sincere himself and he believes he has a government that is good and sincere too. . . . They think, in Britain, that private life and public policy is one seamless garment. Every country has its special illusion. This is the British illusion" (18). To charges of English smugness and self-righteousness, Townrow retorts, "Crap" (19); but the doubt raised remains in his mind and will be decisive, in conjunction with the historical events, in leading to his change of outlook.

In Port Said, Townrow is to be initiated on his quest for identity violently by the physical attack upon him. Newby begins at this point a thorough study of Townrow by reducing him to the "essential human condition"—"naked and hurt" (35). Townrow does not know who he is, nor can he find out. What is there to gauge by? People often take him for somebody else, and he also confuses himself with other people because of his banged memory. Even his nationality is questioned; and, since the police have his passport and do not return it to him until near the end of the novel, he cannot resort to such an official proof of identity.

What is worse, he cannot even authenticate his being a crook. His norm has hitherto always been based on the assumption of the goodness of the British government, and the invalidating of it begun by the travelers in Rome—"why did the [British] government not warn the Jews in Europe?" (16)—is continued by both his presence in Egypt and the aggressive behavior of the British there. Among strangers, he does not know how to evaluate his own behavior. "You find it easier to suspect me of bad faith," he is told, "than you do to believe in the wickedness of your own

government" (155). And with this shake-up comes the disillusionment that the English are "just Bad Men" because they are now
people, like the Kaiser and Hitler, "who start wars and invasions
and commit acts of aggression" (78). Townrow feels "shut out of
Eden" ([166]; the pun on Anthony Eden's name is made evident
here), and his uncertainty then leads him—who "wanted to be in-
formed," "hated bad information," and "wanted to know the
truth" (177)—to the end of his quest. The ending comes in the
form of a redemption: "If the ordinary man did not instinctively
understand the acts of his government and, indeed, found them
bestial he could only respond by taking himself in hand. He must
tell the truth. He must be honest. That was the logic of it.
Otherwise he lost the right to criticize. . . . He just wanted to go
on being a bastard, . . . but, for Christ's sake, how could he if
[Anthony] Eden was one too?" (165).

The third quest provides Townrow, willy-nilly, with a new
ethical code: "You couldn't answer for anything outside your own
personal experience. And if you remembered your own experiences
wrongly you didn't count at all. You weren't human" (186). And he
resolves that "in future he would only answer for himself, and by
God he was going to see it was a simple answer" (233). But, even
so, "You couldn't answer for anybody but yourself and only then if
you were alone" (238).

This quest for identity, it becomes evident, has begotten, along
the way and almost unnoticed, a fourth quest—a quest for a destiny. As a resultant reward of his night-sea journey en route to the
interior and the saint's tomb there, Townrow has been transform-
ed. The experience leads to a new self and a new attitude: "It made
him want to give and to sacrifice himself and to love everybody"
(130). His destiny is not settled at the end of the novel, but Townrow believes that it will be found at "some point near the heart,"
some "clockless retreat" (183). Ever practical, Townrow has been
moving all the while toward this recognition, using his "uncertainty and confusion" as "fuel to lift [him] from the launching
pad" and to drive "him in a marvellous trajectory of hope and
love" (159).

The fifth quest, one lightly scored but nonetheless very important to the hero's change, emerges fully orchestrated at the end of
the novel in Townrow's new self-identity; this quest is for the

father. Townrow realizes that "whenever he ran away he was on course and doing what came easily," and he acknowledges that, "like his father," he is "running away" (283). This acknowledgment confirms at last an identity that Townrow's mother always tried to keep him from making or assuming. As long as he had fought against the father-image and had denied the paternal identity within himself, he had been a victim of his mother's strong-willed machinations and his own deception. But to acknowledge that identity is to find truth and to integrate his personality into a whole and effective agent. Just as his father had deserted his mother, so Townrow refuses to follow Leah at the end. He has now to be alone and to answer for himself: "Women did not like that kind of loneliness" (284).

All the quests—the literal, the moral, the mythic—have thus become one, a quest for truth, "looking at things for what they are" (273). Earlier, Townrow has been caught up in some splendors of insight: "The greatest of these splendours was an assurance that everything would be all right. It was in order to be an optimist. He, personally, was O.K. If you watched long enough you saw that justice was done. . . . [He felt] he'd had time to glance into the way the Universe was organized and see that some good principle operated" (146). These splendors reappear as the dazzle of the sun on the sea in which Townrow is last seen in the little boat; and they also account, in part, for his being there:

Here he was, then, two months later on a tougher escapade than that lake trip. He knew that much more. He had fewer illusions. He now knew he could not afford to surrender the smallest splinter of judgement to any government, organization, cause or campaign. He was to trust only the immediate promptings, what the eye saw, the nose smelled and his hands touched. Nobody again would play him for a sucker about what was right and what was wrong. Nobody but he himself would look after his tender little conscience. This was pride if you like. Arrogance. It was amazing, and ironical, and absurd—he couldn't find the right word—that a lousy crook like himself should creep into middle age thinking of honour. (283–284)

In what surely must be one of the most effective and unforgettable final scenes in modern English fiction, stunning in its imaginative exuberance, Townrow disappears over the horizon. "He was away and alone, stark" (284).

CHAPTER 7

# Postlude

PERHAPS the most impressive aspect of Newby's career as novelist during the period 1945–1968 is the vigor not only of his productivity but of his continual inventiveness. While remaining steadfastly faithful to his theme of love and to the quest for intangible values in the private sphere of personal relationships, he has sought new ways technically to widen scope, to vary mode, and to discover new approaches and angles of vision. One immediate result is that his novels, although sharing in themselves numerous similarities, as do the works of any serious artist, have escaped falling into a predictable repetitiveness.

Beginning with a closed world peopled by characters in elemental, mythic situations, Newby gradually moved his heroes into a closer relationship with the real world, the world of history. The tragical account of Oliver Knight's encountering and experiencing war and madness in *A Step to Silence* and in *The Retreat* marked a climactic intensity of somber mood and technique that was seemingly exhaustive.

In the Egyptian trilogy—*The Picnic at Sakkara, Revolution and Roses*, and *A Guest and His Going*—the mode then became contrastingly comical; and meaning (as well as sheer fun) was derived from the dramatic clash of misunderstanding between not merely different individuals but individuals of different cultures. In these three volumes, comedic technique expanded to include parody and burlesque, and the hero was placed in situations augmented by their inextricable involvement with politics. The hero was now caught in conflicts that were waged between the two worlds which he inhabited, the private and the public. In *One of the Founders* satire became a new mode for the exploration of this dilemma.

Newby displayed in *The Barbary Light* and in *Something to Answer For*, particularly, a remarkable skill in handling the seriocomic—the "truly gay" treatment of the "desperately

126

tragic"—and used public events as a means of scrutinizing the private life, which they both reflected and altered. The earlier heroes—weak, neurotic, but upstanding—now gave way to less admirable men; and the portrait of the irrepressible rogue Townrow in *Something to Answer For* is one of Newby's most praiseworthy achievements.

The novels contain many artistic virtues, not the least considerable of which is the beautifully lean and economical prose. The first sentence of the first novel—"On the third day the land rose out of the sea"—is evidence of Newby's ability to evoke from simple concrete language vibrations and overtones of symbolic significance. Thus this sentence, with its marked visual power of earth rising out of water, announces clearly but unobtrusively the theme of resurrection; and the associative implications of the sentence's key words immediately embody the theme both religiously and mythically. Furthermore, Newby's use of rhythm is uncommonly resourceful. The sentence recounting Townrow's exit at the end of *Something to Answer For*—"He was away and alone, stark" (284)—draws its power from the rhythm. The final word "stark," coming after the regular pulsation of "away and alone," receives emphasized attention as a result of the syncopation which the omission of a second connective "and" creates. "Stark" stresses the theme and the protagonist's situation; the monosyllabically strong word is, moreover, a counterpart of Townrow's brave, new-gained independence.

An overview of the novels also reveals some imperfections. Perhaps the most conspicuous and serious of these, apart from occasionally failing to focus a novel clearly (*Agents and Witnesses, The Snow Pasture, A Guest and His Going*) and becoming burdened down with detail almost to the point of narrative immobility (*A Season in England*), is the overreliance on the mythic pattern. Sometimes this framing device takes the place, and so must do the work, of thoroughgoing analysis and revelation of character in action. A change in character may be visionary, mystical, elusive of literal representation or factual transcription; but such a change is unconvincing if it is merely reported or summarily stated and then announced as a *fait accompli*. Some of the heroes' rebirths, one may say, are more factitiously Caesarean than natural. Such is the case of Hedges, for example, with his fall into the river; and the failure to develop fully that character-change is one of the reasons that *One of the Founders* is a banal and unsuccessful work.

To try to make a final evaluation of the contributions of a writer who is still at work would be premature. Newby has abundantly and repeatedly won the admiration and respect of discriminating readers, fellow writers, and serious critics. In *The Young May Moon, The Retreat, The Picnic at Sakkara* (with the hilarious Muawiya), *The Barbary Light,* and *Something to Answer For* he has proved himself to be the very kind of writer that, in his study of the postwar English novel, he hoped would appear: "a writer to enchant and bedevil us with art."[1] Newby's skill, his intelligence, and his imaginative compassion have earned him and these his five best novels a secure and eminent place in contemporary letters. As Seán O'Faoláin long ago observed of Newby, "No connoisseur of the novel should miss anything from his pen."[2]

# Notes and References

## Chapter One

1. Interview with Bolivar Le Franc, *Books and Bookmen*, XIV (July, 1969), 30.
2. Newby's first publication, a poem, appeared when he was eighteen (Vineta Colby, "P. H. Newby," *Wilson Library Bulletin*, March, 1953, p. 484); two novels written before the war were not published (Terry Coleman, "The Summer of the Seventeenth Novel," *Manchester Guardian Weekly*, May 1, 1969, p. 16).
3. Colby, p. 484.
4. *Twentieth Century Authors:* First Supplement, ed. Stanley J. Kunitz (New York, 1955), p. 712.
5. Coleman, p. 16.
6. "The Novels of Randolph Stow," *Australian Letters*, I (Nov., 1957), 49.
7. Richard Church, "The Deeper War," *John O'London's Weekly*, Feb. 3, 1950, p. 73.
8. Le Franc, p. 32.
9. *Ibid.*
10. Walter Allen, *The Modern Novel in Britain and the United States* (New York, 1964), p. 266.
11. Nona Balakian, "Talk with P. H. Newby," *New York Times Book Review*, April 19, 1953, p. 18. See also Newby's review of Forster's *Two Cheers for Democracy*, "The Art of Remaining Human," *Listener*, Nov. 1, 1951, p. 749.
12. See, e.g., William York Tindall, *Forces in Modern British Literature, 1885-1956* (New York, 1956), p. 107, n. 9: "In *The Picnic at Sakkara* . . . P. H. Newby unites virtues of Waugh, Menen, and Forster"; Robert Gutwilling, "Newby's Precise and Limited Talent," *Commonweal*, Jan. 15, 1960, p. 448: Newby "is the most important and most successful adapter of Mr. Forster's techniques in the art of the novel"; Paul West, *The Modern Novel* (London, 1963), p. 66: "His [Forster's] quiet voice has few heirs: Snow and Angus Wilson; perhaps L. P. Hartley and P. H. Newby (*The Picnic at Sakkara* . . . especially)"; G. S. Fraser, *The Modern Writer and His World*, 3rd ed. (Baltimore, 1964), p. 173: "These books [*The Picnic at*

*Sakkara* and *A Guest and His Going*] are in the tradition of *A Passage to India.*"

13. "A Novelist on His Own," *Times Literary Supplement,* April 6, 1962, p. 232.

14. *Ibid.*

15. See Newby's remark to Nona Balakian, p. 18: "It is much less important today [than in the nineteenth century] to think of the novel simply in terms of characters that are 'alive.' What we really want to know is the 'why' of character. The writer is a myth-maker and his interest goes beyond individual persons."

16. Le Franc, p. 30.

17. *Listener,* April 28, 1949, pp. 721-722. Newby is, of course, drawing upon Shelley's "A Defence of Poetry."

## Chapter Two

1. *The Novel 1945-1950* (London, 1951), pp. 40, 24.

2. Ephesians, 4:21-25.

3. Possible thematic implications of the name Pierre Bartas are fascinating. Pierre ("stone"), because of his self-centered nature, is unresponsive and unyielding like a stone; he would like to be able to work in stone (i.e., to make of his own life an artwork of form and meaning), but he lacks the "craft"—"Oh, to go to work on a mountain of granite and release the limbs of the angels imprisoned there!" (22); he is a rolling stone in his quests for money and meaning; the reader thinks ironically of the parable of the one who, asking for bread, would not be given a stone; etc. *Bartas,* pronounced much like *barter,* suggests trade and mercenariness, hence mammon, false value, venality.

4. Debasement and absence of love are conspicuous in Sankilos. See: "Does nobody marry for love? he thought. . . . Money, of course" (49); "Nobody understands love these days. . . . The only people who understand love are the whores" (51).

## Chapter Three

1. *The Novel,* pp. 25, 24.

2. Both of these novels deal explicit with the theme of good versus evil. *The Spirit of Jem* (1947), the better work, is an oddly sophisticated tale of adventure and mystery that is also an obvious moral and political allegory. It employs some of Newby's persistent characteristics: the bewildered hero; dreamlikeness; mythical elements; the themes of identity and appearance and reality. The young protagonist is the first-person narrator. He has lost his memory and begins his story with the disarming

statement, "I did not know where I was." He soon becomes involved with Jem, a devilish redheaded boy whose "spirit" is a will to power. Jem is one of a gang who plan to take over the world and who use the milk supply to affect, and thus gain control over, the people's minds.

The action of *The Loot Runners* (1949) also takes place in a bad-dream world. It is narrated in the first person, often rather awkwardly, by both young Bill McQueen and his father. They and a rich Egyptian pasha, who has come to England to purchase a yacht, encounter and eventually put down a group of thieves and jewel smugglers. The work has in common with *The Young May Moon* (published the following year) several thematic and technical features; even the character-name Rice occurs in both novels. For Newby's comments on the subject of children and adolescence in modern literature, see "The Muse in the Nursery," *Listener*, Aug. 5, 1948, pp. 203-204, and *The Novel*, pp. 8 ff.

3. See Northrop Frye, *Anatomy of Criticism* (Princeton, 1957), pp. 163 ff.

4. "Shades of Lawrence and Freud!" remarks Fred of Mariner (16). The phrase also very aptly describes the intricate psychological relationships of members of the Paul family. Mr. Paul has a fatherly preference for Gladys, a fact that may be basically responsible for Fred's having shot his sister because of his jealousy. Gladys says the shooting was an accident, to which Fred replies, "Nothing is purely accidental" (41). (This situation and this comment have strong resemblances to Gerald's accidental shooting of his brother and to Birkin's disbelief in accidents in Lawrence's *Women in Love*, the influence of which is in many ways evident in this novel.)

Mr. Paul's frequent admonitions that Fred should marry indicate his desire to have the son out of the way so that he can have his daughter and his wife to himself. When Mary comes to their house, both father and son are attracted to her; and the father even urges the son to take her away from Mariner, as he says he would do if younger. Mary falls in love with Fred, but to assuage Gladys's jealousy Fred tells her he "never had any feelings for Mary in the way she thinks" (222). Mrs. Paul notes with jealousy that her husband has "taken a fancy" to Mary, and her "sympathies" turn "just a little" against the girl (143, 156).

5. Fred has a sickly younger brother, Tom, who hardly figures in the novel except to precipitate an argument between Fred and his father. Evidently the reader is to infer, from Mr. Paul's statement that the family name can live on only through Fred, that Tom will die before maturity.

6. The name Gladys may derive from *gladiole*, a flower; if so, it further supports her symbolic connection with spring.

7. George D. Painter, "New Novels," *Listener*, Feb. 10, 1949, p. 240.

8. "The Classical Manner," *Times Literary Supplement*, Jan. 22, 1949, p. 53.

9. *The Novel*, p. 9.

10. See Lucia Dickerson, "Portrait of the Artist as a Jung Man," *Kenyon Review*, XXI (Winter, 1959), 62-63.

11. Adrian and Grainger are, along with Rice and Philip, also thematically unified and collapsed into one male figure by their relationship with Laura. Adrian, Rice's brother, had been in love with her and had first introduced her to Grainger. Reflecting this male-female relationship on a lower, comic level is a subplot dealing with Adrian's helpers at the bakehouse, Ivor and Mari (who, like Laura, has supernatural associations).

12. *New Statesman and Nation*, Jan. 21, 1950, p. 75.

### Chapter Four

1. Allen, *The Modern Novel*, p. 266.

2. Harvey Curtis Webster, "Bloomsbury in Austerity," *Saturday Review*, May 2, 1953, p. 30—but see Webster's later opinion in *After the Trauma: Representative British Novelists Since 1920* (Lexington, Ky., 1970), pp. 192-193, that Newby "has not realized the promise of *Journey into the Interior* [*sic*] (1945), though *Barbary Light* [*sic*] (1962) comes close." See also Anthony West, "Two Cheers," *New Yorker*, May 9, 1953, pp. 130, 132.

3. Allen, pp. 266-267; Anthony Burgess, *The Novel Now* (New York, 1967), p. 68. John McCormick's claim in *Catastrophe and Imagination* (London, 1957), p. 166, that these two novels are "better novels than anything of Virginia Woolf or D. H. Lawrence" is extreme.

4. Allen, p. 266.

5. *Ibid.*, p. 267.

### Chapter Five

1. The sequential publication of the Egyptian trilogy was interrupted by the appearance of *Ten Miles from Anywhere* (1958), a volume of nineteen not particularly distinguished short stories, all of which had originally appeared in English and American magazines. According to the prefatory editorial note, the book has two "main strands": Oriental and fantastic, English and lyric. But this statement is slightly misleading because it suggests a unity that the collection lacks.

What is notable about the volume is the different kinds of stories, which "range far and wide in human emotions," as one reviewer commented ("Passion and Regret," *Times Literary Supplement*, June 13, 1958, p. 334). F. X. Mathews, in "Newby on the Nile: The Comic Trilogy," *Twentieth*

*Century Literature*, XIV (April, 1968), 15-16, n. 6, has pointed out that one story, "Promotion," is "an unabashed borrowing" of "The Chief of the Old Cairo Police," which appears in Newby's edition of *Tales from the Arabian Nights*.

2. Coleman, "Summer of the Seventeenth Novel," p. 16.

3. "Having Drunk of the Nile," *Listener*, Feb. 24, 1949, pp. 307-308. Newby's interest in the Middle East is further evidenced in "Profile of a Lady of Mystery" (*New York Times Magazine*, Sept. 18, 1949, pp. 24-25, 64, 66), an essay on Cleopatra, and in introductions he wrote for editions of A. W. Kinglake's *Eothen* (1948) and *The Book of the Thousand and One Nights* (1950); a shorter version of the second introduction appeared in the *Listener*, Jan. 29, 1948, pp. 178-179. Several of the stories in *Ten Miles from Anywhere* have Oriental settings and characters, and two characters in *The Loot Runners* are Egyptians.

4. Violent attacks involving individual Easterners and Westerners occur in each novel of the trilogy: an assassination attempt in *The Picnic at Sakkara;* a face slap and a spit in the face in *Revolution and Roses;* another face slap and an attempted murder with a poisoned dart in *A Guest and His Going.*

5. See "Written in Sand," a piece Newby published in the *New Statesman and Nation*, April 12, 1947, pp. 251-252; it is a kind of nuclear sketch of this novel.

6. Matthews, "Newby on the Nile," p. 8.

7. Norman Podhoretz, "Opéra Bouffe on the Nile," *New Yorker*, July 27, 1957, p. 69.

8. In all three novels the telephone is used to extremely comic purpose as a device of commenting ironically on the theme of communication. Characters repeatedly have difficulty with the instrument: lines are tapped, wires are cut, false names are given by callers and answers, characters eavesdrop on one another, important calls are delayed because of lack of proper coins for pay-stations, etc.

9. Fraser, *The Modern Writer*, p. 174.

10. Mathews, p. 14, has suggested that Hillingdon's possession might well be read on the level of political allegory as "the subversion of the English consciousness by the irrational reality of Egypt."

11. Francis Wyndham, review of *The Picnic at Sakkara*, *London Magazine*, II (July, 1955), 80: "All of P. H. Newby's novels have been distinguished by a quality that can be vaguely defined as taste, but his latest has a good deal more; his gifts, always apparent, have suddenly been placed in correct proportion to each other, and the result is an individual success."

12. *The Present Age in British Literature* (Bloomington, Ind., 1958),

p. 322: *"The Picnic at Sakkara* is a brilliant comic novel, combining criticism and compassion, irony and affection, in an unusual and most effective manner."

13. Le Franc, interview in *Books and Bookmen*, p. 30: "It [*The Picnic at Sakkara*] owed a great deal to Forster's *A Passage to India*. Indeed Forster's attitude to the East is something I suppose has made a deep impression on me. Certainly *Picnic at Sakkara* could not have been written but for the way Forster had written *A Passage to India*."

14. James Hall, however, omits Newby from his study *The Tragic Comedians: Seven Modern British Novelists* (Bloomington, Ind., 1963) because, in his opinion, Newby is "thinner" than Forster, Huxley, Waugh, Cary, Green, L. P. Hartley, and Anthony Powell and because "his dramatic conflicts cut less deeply" than theirs. But he admits nonetheless that Newby, along with Ivy Compton-Burnett, has "comic talents which, in an age less loaded with these, would be outstanding" (p. v).

## Chapter Six

1. "Prizewinner," *Listener*, April 24, 1969, p. 567.

2. "A Novelist on His Own," p. 232.

3. "In England's Green and Pleasant Land," *New Republic*, Oct. 30, 1965, pp. 23-25.

4. "Victims of Circumstance," *New Yorker*, Dec. 25, 1965, p. 62.

5. *Ibid.*

6. The American edition (Philadelphia and New York, 1969) corrects various discrepancies in the English edition and is therefore the preferred text of *Something to Answer For*.

7. Le Franc, interview in *Books and Bookmen*, p. 31.

8. For this novel Newby received early in 1969 the *Yorkshire Post* Fiction Award. More importantly, for this same novel he became a few months later the first recipient of the Booker Fiction Prize, financially the most substantial literary award in Great Britain (£5,000, tax-free). From a short list including *The Nice and the Good* by Iris Murdoch, *The Public Image* by Muriel Spark, *Impossible Object* by Nicholas Mosley, *From Scenes like These* by Gordon M. Williams, and *Figures in a Landscape* by Barry England, *Something to Answer For* was the unanimous choice of the selection committee, of which three members were Rebecca West, Stephen Spender, and Frank Kermode. The adjudicators praised Newby's novel for "its vision, its concreteness and its finely articulate energy" ("First Booker Fiction Prize Award," *Bookseller*, April 26, 1969, p. 2213).

9. It is instructive to note the extent to which certain aspects and details of Townrow's experience duplicate Owen's in *The Barbary Light*.

10. In a very perceptive review of this novel ("Double Deal," *New*

*Yorker*, Sept. 6, 1969, pp. 125-128), Wilfrid Sheed identifies in it a political allegory with the British Empire as a "vague, *de-facto* scoundrel": "As Townrow-England's designs on old lady-colony go astray, he turns to helping her instead, but on terms he thinks best for her. On the way, he has an affair with a girl who could very well be Israel, etc."

11. All of Newby's remarks about this novel are to be found in "Prizewinner" and Le Franc.

12. Time past balances repetitively with time present, too. During his first stay in Egypt, Townrow fell on his head and met the Khourys; a return, due to the Khourys, leads to another head accident.

13. *Random House Dictionary of the English Language* (New York, 1967), p. 572.

*Chapter Seven*

1. *The Novel*, p. 7.
2. "New Novels," *Listener*, April 17, 1952, p. 645.

# Selected Bibliography

PRIMARY SOURCES

1. Fiction

*A Journey to the Interior.* London: Jonathan Cape, 1945; Garden City: Doubleday, 1946.

*Agents and Witnesses.* London: Jonathan Cape, 1947; Garden City: Doubleday, 1947.

*The Spirit of Jem.* London: John Lehmann, 1947; New York: Delacorte Press, 1967.

*Mariner Dances.* London: Jonathan Cape, 1948.

*The Snow Pasture.* London: Jonathan Cape, 1949.

*The Loot Runners.* London: John Lehmann, 1949.

*The Young May Moon.* London: Jonathan Cape, 1950; New York: Alfred A. Knopf, 1951.

*A Season in England.* London: Jonathan Cape, 1951; New York: Alfred A. Knopf, 1952.

*A Step to Silence.* London: Jonathan Cape, 1952.

*The Retreat.* London: Jonathan Cape, 1953; New York: Alfred A. Knopf, 1953.

*The Picnic at Sakkara.* London: Jonathan Cape, 1955; New York: Alfred A. Knopf, 1955.

*Revolution and Roses.* London: Jonathan Cape, 1957; New York: Alfred A. Knopf, 1957.

*Ten Miles from Anywhere and Other Stories.* London: Jonathan Cape, 1958. Contents: "Uncle Kevork," "The Beginning of Exile," "Lament on the Death of a Donkey," "Khamseen," "Promotion," "The China Tomato," "A Parcel for Alexandria," "The Baker's Daughter," "The Song," "Ten Miles from Anywhere," "A Glass of Water," "Mr. Cornibeer," "A Man of Taste," "Palmer," "The Pioneer," "An Unrecorded Interview," "The Man from Barcelona," "The Heat of Texas," "A Grove in Syria."

*A Guest and His Going.* London: Jonathan Cape, 1959; New York: Alfred A. Knopf, 1959.

*The Barbary Light.* London: Faber & Faber, 1962; Philadelphia and New York: Lippincott, 1964.

*One of the Founders.* London: Faber & Faber, 1965; Philadelphia and New
York: Lippincott, 1965.
*Something to Answer For.* London: Faber & Faber, 1968; Philadelphia and
New York: Lippincott, 1969.

2. Selected List of Other Works

"The Achievement of Maria Edgeworth," *Listener,* June 9, 1949, pp. 986-
987.
*The Book of the Thousand and One Nights.* By Sir Richard Burton. Edited
with introduction by Newby. London: Arthur Barker, 1950; New York:
Pocket Books [1959], under the title *Tales from the Arabian Nights.*
"The Good Sailor," *London Magazine,* VI (Dec., 1959), 13-25. A story.
"Grimm's Fairy Spell," *Listener,* Dec. 23, 1948, pp. 978-979.
"Having Drunk of the Nile," *Listener,* Feb. 24, 1949, pp. 307-308.
Introduction. *Eothen.* By A. W. Kinglake. London: John Lehmann, 1948.
*Maria Edgeworth.* London: Arthur Barker, 1950; Denver: Alan Swallow,
1950.
"The Muse in the Nursery," *Listener,* Aug. 5, 1958, pp. 203-204. A slightly
shorter version: "The Changing Mood of the Muse in the Nursery,"
*New York Times Book Review,* March 5, 1950, pp. 7, 16.
*The Novel 1945-1950.* London: Longmans, Green, 1951.
"The Novels of Randolph Stow," *Australian Letters,* I (Nov., 1957), 49-51.
"Profile of a Lady of Mystery," *New York Times Magazine,* Sept. 18, 1949,
pp. 24-25, 64, 66. On Cleopatra.
"The Sea and the Savage," *Listener,* Sept. 20, 1951, pp. 457-458. On
Fenimore Cooper.
"The 'Thousand and One Nights,' " *Listener,* Jan. 29, 1948, pp. 178-179.
"The West Wycombe of Baron le Despenser," *Listener,* Jan. 20, 1949,
pp. 94-96.
"The World of Imagination," *Listener,* April 28, 1949, pp. 721-722.
"Written in Sand," *New Statesman and Nation,* April 12, 1947, pp. 251-
252.

3. Selected List of Reviews

"The Art of Remaining Human" [*Two Cheers for Democracy,* by E. M.
Forster], *Listener,* Nov. 1, 1951, p. 749.
"Book Reviews" [*Roman Tales,* by Alberto Moravia; *The Presence of
Grace,* by J. F. Powers; et al.], *London Magazine,* IV (May, 1957), 79-
87.
"Book Reviews" [*Collected Short Stories,* by Aldous Huxley; et al.], *Lon-
don Magazine,* IV (Sept., 1957), 65-69.

"Book Reviews" [*Black Midas*, by Jan Carew; *The Suffrage of Elvira*, by V. S. Naipaul; *Ways of Sunlight*, by Samuel Selvon], *London Magazine*, V (Nov., 1958), 82-84.

"Book Reviews" [*Our Man in Havana*, by Graham Greene], *London Magazine*, V (Dec., 1958), 65-67.

"Indian Children" [*And Gazelles Leaping*, by Sudhin N. Ghose], *New Statesman and Nation*, March 19, 1949, pp. 283-284.

"An Intellectual Wobble" [*But to What Purpose*, by E. L. Grant Watson], *New Statesman and Nation*, March 29, 1947, pp. 218-219.

"New Novels" [*Manservant and Maidservant*, by I. Compton-Burnett; *Teresa*, by Seán O'Faoláin; et al.], *New Statesman and Nation*, March 15, 1947, p. 182.

"New Novels" [*Eustace and Hilda*, by L. P. Hartley; *Innocents*, by A. L. Barker; et al.], *Listener*, Aug. 7, 1947, p. 232.

"New Novels" [*Insh'allah*, by H. M. Webb; et al.], *Listener*, Sept. 4, 1947, p. 404.

"New Novels" [*A View of the Harbour*, by Elizabeth Taylor; *The Museum of Cheats*, by Sylvia Townsend Warner; et al.], *Listener*, Oct. 16, 1947, p. 693.

"New Novels" [*Cefalû*, by Lawrence Durrell; *The Bulwark*, by Theodore Dreiser; et al.], *New Statesman and Nation*, March 6, 1948, pp. 197-198.

"New Novels" [*Growing Up*, by Olivia Manning; *Never Again*, by Francis King; et al.], *New Statesman and Nation*, May 29, 1948, pp. 440-441.

"New Novels" [*Bernard Clayre*, by James T. Farrell; et al.], *New Statesman and Nation*, July 17, 1948, p. 57.

"New Novels" [*Doctor Faustus*, by Thomas Mann; *The City and the Pillar*, by Gore Vidal; et al.], *Listener*, May 5, 1949, p. 774.

"New Novels" [*The Naked and the Dead*, by Norman Mailer; *The Body*, by William Sansom; et al.], *Listener*, May 19, 1949, p. 862.

"New Novels" [*All Things Betray Thee*, by Gwyn Thomas; et al.], *Listener*, June 2, 1949, p. 949.

"New Novels" [*Nineteen Eighty-Four*, by George Orwell; *Conversation in Italy*, by Elio Vittorini; *Hunting the Fairies*, by Compton Mackenzie], *Listener*, June 16, 1949, p. 1036.

"New Novels" [*Two Worlds and Their Ways*, by I. Compton-Burnett; et al.], *Listener*, July 7, 1949, p. 36.

"New Novels" [*The Woman of Rome*, by Alberto Moravia; *The Grand Design*, by John Dos Passos; et al.], *Listener*, July 14, 1949, p. 80.

"New Novels" [*The River Line*, by Charles Morgan; et al.], *Listener*, July 28, 1949, p. 162.

"New Short Stories" [*Creatures of Circumstance*, by W. Somerset

Maugham; *Nineteen Stories*, by Graham Greene; et al.], *Listener*,
Aug. 21, 1947, p. 316.
"Personal Remarks" [*The Short Story*, by Seán O'Faoláin], *New Statesman
and Nation*, Dec. 25, 1948, pp. 575-576.
"Ruins and Splendours" [*Syria*, by Robin Fedden], *Listener*, Oct. 17, 1946,
p. 528.
"Strong, Sincere, Sad" [*Arnold Bennett*, by Walter Allen], *New Statesman
and Nation*, Nov. 6, 1948, p. 400.

SECONDARY SOURCES

ALLEN, WALTER. *The Modern Novel in Britain and the United States.*
New York: Dutton, 1964; London: Phoenix House, 1964, under the title *Tradition and Dream.* Contains a brief commentary on the two
related novels about Oliver Knight through which "Newby is probably
best approached."
Anon. "A Novelist on His Own," *Times Literary Supplement*, April 6,
1962, p. 232. Reprinted in *T.L.S. 1962.* London: Oxford University
Press, 1963. Essay-review of *The Barbary Light*; also includes
trenchant survey of all of Newby's fiction.
————. "Prizewinner," *Listener*, April 24, 1969, p. 567. Important as a
transcript of some remarks by Newby on *Something to Answer For.*
BALAKIAN, NONA. "Talk with P. H. Newby," *New York Times Book
Review*, April 19, 1953, p. 18. Comments by Newby on personal attitudes and literary influences.
BUFKIN, E. C. "Quest in the Novels of P. H. Newby," *Critique*, VIII
(Fall, 1965), 51-62. Discussion of the quest theme in three novels.
BURGESS, ANTHONY. *The Novel Now: A Guide to Contemporary Fiction.* New York: Norton, 1967. Passing attention to Newby in a chapter
entitled "Good and Evil." Sees his best novels as about a "fundamental bewilderment — that of man himself, lost in a desert without a
compass."
COLBY, VINETA. " P. H. Newby," *Wilson Library Bulletin*, March, 1953,
p. 484. Reprinted in *Current Biography 1953*, pp. 456-457. Contains
biographical information.
COLEMAN, TERRY. "The Summer of the Seventeenth Novel," *Manchester Guardian Weekly*, May 1, 1969, p. 16. Reported interview important for Newby's comments.
DICKERSON, LUCIA. "Portrait of the Artist as a Jung Man," *Kenyon
Review*, XXI (Winter, 1959), 58-83. Important discussion of Jungian
concepts as both the basis of Newby's novels and the source of their
obscurity, as shown in complicated and recondite analyses of *The
Snow Pasture* and *The Young May Moon.*

FRASER, G. S. *The Modern Writer and His World.* 3rd ed. Baltimore: Penguin Books, 1964. Brief discussion of *The Picnic at Sakkara* and *A Guest and His Going,* which "deserve to be minor classics." Says Newby "is hard to match among his contemporaries" for "sheer professionalism" and "competent and patient attention to the novel as an economical art."

KARL, FREDERICK R. *The Contemporary English Novel.* New York: Farrar, Straus & Cudahy, 1962. Discusses Newby along with William Golding, Iris Murdoch, and Rex Warner in a chapter on the novel as moral allegory. Generally depreciative; says that, despite his high reputation, "Newby's is a small talent" and that his novels "lack vitality and intensity."

LE FRANC, BOLIVAR. Interview with P. H. Newby, *Books and Bookmen,* XIV (July, 1969), 30-32. Extremely valuable comments on background and some of the novels.

MC CORMICK, JOHN. *Catastrophe and Imagination: An Interpretation of the Recent English and American Novel.* London: Longmans, Green, 1957. Contains several short but perceptive and enthusiastic passages about Newby's work, which "characterizes the best that has occurred in post-World War II English fiction."

MATHEWS, F. X. "The Fiction of P. H. Newby." Unpublished dissertation, University of Wisconsin, 1964. Very resourceful, enlightening study. Includes passages from two letters from Newby and from an unpublished essay by him, "Catching Time by the Tail."

———. "Newby on the Nile: The Comic Trilogy," *Twentieth Century Literature,* XIV (April, 1968), 3-16. Excellent, thorough critical analysis of the Egyptian trilogy.

———. "Witness to Violence: The War Novels of P. H. Newby," *Texas Studies in Literature and Language,* XII (Spring, 1970), 121-135. Skillful study of *A Step to Silence* and *The Retreat.*

POSS, STANLEY. "Manners and Myths in the Novels of P. H. Newby," *Critique,* XII (1970), 5-19. Analyses of *A Journey to the Interior* and *A Season in England* that illustrate "the variety of [Newby's] fictional strategies as well as the essential unity of his vision." Asserts that Newby's best novels rank collectively "as one of the most substantial achievements in English fiction during the last two decades." Contains a comment on Jung quoted from a letter from Newby.

QUINTON, ANTHONY, et al. "The New Novelists: An Enquiry," *London Magazine,* V (Nov., 1958), 13-31. Symposium by four distinguished critics; Newby often mentioned and work evaluated with that of other postwar English novelists. Contains interesting comparison of Newby and Francis King.

*Twentieth Century Authors.* First Supplement. Ed. Stanley J. Kunitz. New York: H. W. Wilson, 1955. Contains biographical information.

WATTS, HAROLD H. "P. H. Newby: Experience as Farce," *Perspective*, X (Summer-Autumn, 1958), 106-117. Interesting consideration of Newby's novels, comical or tragical, as depicting the farcical inconsequence of experience within character and without.

WEST, PAUL, *The Modern Novel.* London: Hutchinson, 1963. No extended attention devoted to Newby, but he is grouped with such novelists as Anthony Burgess, Rex Warner, Rayner Heppenstall, Gabriel Fielding, and William Sansom who deal with "the poetic, the subjective and the metaphysical" as opposed to the writers of "class-picaresque."

# Index

(The works of Newby are listed under his name)